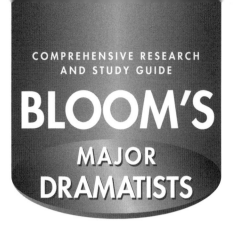

COMPREHENSIVE RESEARCH
AND STUDY GUIDE

BLOOM'S
MAJOR
DRAMATISTS

Ben
Jonson

EDITED AND WITH AN
INTRODUCTION BY HAROLD BLOOM

BLOOM'S MAJOR DRAMATISTS

Aeschylus

Anton Chekhov

Aristophanes

Berthold Brecht

Euripides

Henrik Ibsen

Ben Jonson

Christopher Marlowe

Arthur Miller

Eugene O'Neill

Shakespeare's Comedies

Shakespeare's Histories

Shakespeare's Romances

Shakespeare's Tragedies

George Bernard Shaw

Neil Simon

Sophocles

Tennessee Williams

August Wilson

BLOOM'S MAJOR NOVELISTS

Jane Austen

The Brontës

Willa Cather

Stephen Crane

Charles Dickens

Fyodor Dostoevsky

William Faulkner

F. Scott Fitzgerald

Thomas Hardy

Nathaniel Hawthorne

Ernest Hemingway

Henry James

James Joyce

D. H. Lawrence

Toni Morrison

John Steinbeck

Stendhal

Leo Tolstoy

Mark Twain

Alice Walker

Edith Wharton

Virginia Woolf

BLOOM'S MAJOR WORLD POETS

Geoffrey Chaucer

Emily Dickinson

John Donne

T. S. Eliot

Robert Frost

Langston Hughes

John Milton

Edgar Allan Poe

Shakespeare's Poems & Sonnets

Alfred, Lord Tennyson

Walt Whitman

William Wordsworth

BLOOM'S MAJOR SHORT STORY WRITERS

William Faulkner

F. Scott Fitzgerald

Ernest Hemingway

O. Henry

James Joyce

Herman Melville

Flannery O'Connor

Edgar Allan Poe

J. D. Salinger

John Steinbeck

Mark Twain

Eudora Welty

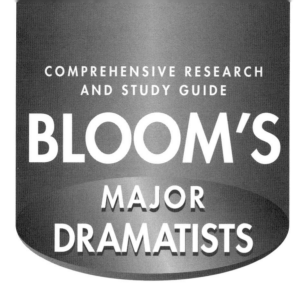

COMPREHENSIVE RESEARCH
AND STUDY GUIDE

BLOOM'S
MAJOR
DRAMATISTS

Ben Jonson

EDITED AND WITH AN INTRODUCTION
BY HAROLD BLOOM

First Printing
1 3 5 7 9 8 6 4 2

Library of Congress Cataloging-in-Publication Data
Ben Jonson / edited and with an introduction by Harold Bloom.
        p. cm. — (Bloom's major dramatists)
        ISBN 0-7910-6359-3 (alk. paper)
        1. Jonson, Ben, 1573?–1967—Criticism and interpretation.
        I. Bloom, Harold. II. Title. III. Series.

        PR2638 .B46 2001
        822'.3—dc21   2001053677

Chelsea House Publishers
1974 Sproul Road, Suite 400
Broomall, PA 19008-0914

The Chelsea House World Wide Web address is
http://www.chelseahouse.com

Series Editor: Matt Uhler

Contributing Editor: Tara Mohr

Produced by Publisher's Services, Santa Barbara, California

Contents

User's Guide

This volume is designed to present biographical, critical, and bibliographical information on the author's best-known or most important works. Following Harold Bloom's editor's note and introduction is a detailed biography of the author, discussing major life events and important literary accomplishments. A plot summary of each play follows, tracing significant themes, patterns, and motifs in the work.

A selection of critical extracts, derived from previously published material from leading critics, analyzes aspects of each play. The extracts consist of statements from the author, if available, early reviews of the work, and later evaluations up to the present. A bibliography of the author's writings (including a complete list of all works written, cowritten, edited, and translated), a list of additional books and articles on the author and his or her work, and an index of themes and ideas in the author's writings conclude the volume.

~

Harold Bloom is Sterling Professor of the Humanities at Yale University and Henry W. and Albert A. Berg Professor of English at the New York University Graduate School. He is the author of over 20 books, including *Shelley's Mythmaking* (1959), *The Visionary Company* (1961), *Blake's Apocalypse* (1963), *Yeats* (1970), *A Map of Misreading* (1975), *Kabbalah and Criticism* (1975), *Agon: Toward a Theory of Revisionism* (1982), *The American Religion* (1992), *The Western Canon* (1994), and *Omens of Millennium: The Gnosis of Angels, Dreams, and Resurrection* (1996). *The Anxiety of Influence* (1973) sets forth Professor Bloom's provocative theory of the literary relationships between the great writers and their predecessors. His most recent books include *Shakespeare: The Invention of the Human*, a 1998 National Book Award finalist, and *How to Read and Why*, which was published in 2000.

Professor Bloom earned his Ph.D. from Yale University in 1955 and has served on the Yale faculty since then. He is a 1985 MacArthur Foundation Award recipient, served as the Charles Eliot Norton Professor of Poetry at Harvard University in 1987–88, and has received honorary degrees from the universities of Rome and Bologna. In 1999, Professor Bloom received the prestigious American Academy of Arts and Letters Gold Medal for Criticism.

Currently, Harold Bloom is the editor of numerous Chelsea House volumes of literary criticism, including the series BLOOM'S NOTES, BLOOM'S MAJOR DRAMATISTS, BLOOM'S MAJOR NOVELISTS, MAJOR LITERARY CHARACTERS, MODERN CRITICAL VIEWS, MODERN CRITICAL INTERPRETATIONS, and WOMEN WRITERS OF ENGLISH AND THEIR WORKS.

Editor's Note

My Introduction contrasts Shakespeare's creation of personalities to Jonson's art of satiric ideograms, and then turns to *Volpone* as Jonson's triumph in his own mode.

Critical views commence with the poet Algernon Charles Swinburne, who implicitly reminds us that, for Ben Jonson, art was hard work. On *Every Man in His Humour,* William Hazlitt observes that the play acts better than it reads, after which Anne Barton illuminates Jonson's revisions, and Simon Trussler discusses issues of comic characterization. David Riggs discusses Jonson's use of Galen's four humours, while Robert N. Watson's focus is on pretense and realism.

On *Volpone,* Herford and Simpson see Jonson's severity as approaching tragedy, after which Jonson himself addresses his moral purposes in the play. Alvin B. Kernan audaciously suggests that the mountebank Scoto of Mantua, whom Volpone impersonates, is Jonson's own mask as satirist, while Una Mary Ellis-Fermor subtly indicates Jonson's own affection for Volpone. Leo Salingar finds the quest for an elixir of life in Volpone's antics, after which Jonas A. Barish defends the relevance of the sub-plot, and the great critic William Empson speculates upon Volpone's vitalism.

On *The Alchemist,* Swinburne returns to compare the play to *Volpone,* confessing his equal love for both. The Romantic poet critic, S. T. Coleridge, praises Jonson's originality, while Herford and Simpson interestingly contrast Subtle and Face with Volpone and Mosca. Kernan finds an analogue to alchemy in Jonson's own poetic wit, after which the poet-critic John Dryden sees Shakespeare as Homer, with Jonson as Virgil. Ian Donaldson analyzes timing in *The Alchemist,* showing how Jonson utilizes it as a source of meaning.

On *Bartholomew Fair,* Jonson himself says his art embraces wit while repudiating low comedy, while Herford and Simpson find the fair to be the play's center, and Harry Levin contrasts Jonson's realism to Shakespeare's. Eugene Waith describes and praises Jonson's innovations after which Edward B. Partridge examines Jonson's satire of contemporary lawgivers. Ian Donaldson subtly discusses Jonson's strategy of both appeasing and criticizing his audience, while Richard Allen Cave centers upon the puppet-play scene.

Introduction

HAROLD BLOOM

I

Ben Jonson, Shakespeare's friend and rival, owed his start as a dramatist to Shakespeare's generosity in bringing Jonson to the notice of the Lord Chamberlain's Men, Shakespeare's players, in 1598. Jonson, pugnacious and furiously learned, from 1599 on asserted himself to become almost the anti-Shakespeare in his dramas. In effect, Jonson challenged Shakespeare for the heritage of Christopher Marlowe. There is considerable irony in this, since Marlowe had no comic invention, while Jonson survives now only for his comedies, *Volpone* and *The Alchemist* in particular. T. S. Eliot shrewdly saw Jonson as Marlowe's continuator, which is peculiarly true in the sense that Marlowe's characters all are cartoons, and Jonson's, when successful, all are caricatures. The disasters of Jonson's *Sejanus,* his major tragedy, and of *Catiline,* his later attempt to outdo Shakespeare in Roman tragedy, are instructive, despite the noble obfuscations of Eliot, which are sublimely mistaken:

> The creation of a work of art, we will say the creation of a character in a drama, consists in the process of transfusion of the personality, or, in a deeper sense, the life, of the author into the character. This is a very different matter from the orthodox creation in one's own image. The ways in which the passions and desires of the creator may be satisfied in the work of art are complex and devious. In a painter they may take the form of a predilection for certain colours, tones, or lightings; in a writer the original impulse may be even more strangely transmuted. Now, we may say with Mr. Gregory Smith that Falstaff or a score of Shakespeare's characters have a "third dimension" that Jonson's have not. This will mean, not that Shakespeare's spring from the feelings or imagination and Jonson's from the intellect or invention; they have equally an emotional source; but that Shakespeare's represent a more complex tissue of feelings and desires, as well as a more supple, a more susceptible temperament. Falstaff is not only the roast Manningtree ox with the pudding in his belly; he also "grows old," and, finally, his nose is as sharp as a pen. He

was perhaps the satisfaction of more, and of more complicated feelings; and perhaps he was, as the great tragic characters must have been, the offspring of deeper, less apprehensible feelings: deeper, but not necessarily stronger or more intense, than those of Jonson. It is obvious that the spring of the difference is not the difference between feeling and thought, or superior insight, superior perception, on the part of Shakespeare, but his susceptibility to a greater range of emotion, and emotion deeper and more obscure. But his characters are no more "alive" than are the characters of Jonson.

What *are* "deeper, but not necessarily stronger or more intense" feelings? Unless Eliot (who despised Freud) intends another disparagement of depth psychology, he evades coherence here. Are Falstaff and Cleopatra, Hamlet and Iago, Lear and Macbeth really no more "alive" than Volpone and Mosca, Morose and Truewit, Subtle and Sir Epicure Mammon?

Jonson, like Marlowe, does not attempt to give us representations of human inwardness. Marlowe overwhelms us with rhetorical splendor, while Jonson's satirical comedy also employs stunning eloquence rather than insights into the mysteries of personality. At their best, roles in Jonson are ideograms. In his Prologue to *Cynthia's Revels*, Jonson said that his kind of play "affords/ Words above action: matter, above words." This is directed against Shakespeare, who lacked "matter," in Jonson's sense of moral instruction. And yet the matter of Jonson's "comical satires"—*Every Man Out of His Humour, Cynthia's Revels,* and *Poetaster*—essentially is Jonson's self-love, and his assertion that he alone is the Poet. Time, despite T. S. Eliot's neo-classical last stand, has settled the matter. We stage and read *Twelfth Night,* and not *Cynthia's Revels.*

Canonization is now an absurdly abused process, but is simply a question of just how much time any of us have. I enjoy *Cynthia's Revels,* such as it is, but it is food for specialists. The California School system now insists upon multiculturalism, but by this it is not meant that students are to read *The Tale of Genji* and *Don Quixote,* but rather recent works of Japanese-American and Hispanic-American origin. If we were all to live three hundred years, rather than seventy-five, this might be admirable. If not, not.

The best account of the wit-combat between Shakespeare and Jonson is in *Shakespeare and The Poets' War* by James P. Bednarz (2001). Bednarz demonstrates Shakespeare's counter-measures against Jonson in *As You Like It, Twelfth Night,* and *Troilus and Cressida,* comedies that deftly satirize the satirical Jonson.

Ben Jonson is a great lyric and reflective poet, but he achieves the heights as a dramatic poet only in *Volpone* and *The Alchemist,* where the critique of Shakespeare is very indirect. Jonson satirizes sexual desire, and the satire is without limits. Shakespeare both satirizes and exalts desire in his comedies through *Twelfth Night,* and then turns against it (though with ironic reservations) in the final comedies: *Troilus and Cressida, All's Well that Ends Well,* and *Measure for Measure.* Jonson, who could not get away from Shakespeare in tragedy—his attempt to write a rival *Richard III* was abandoned—created a mode of comedy that was all his own, and that clearly possesses a moral purpose. Shakespeare happily fled from Jonsonian moral purposes, as they were antithetical to any adequately complex vision of Eros. Shakespeare, like Marlowe, was an Ovidian poet; Jonson preferred Horace. And yet, by temperament, Jonson was exuberant and vehement, "burly Ben." His masterpiece is *Volpone,* which is—akin to Shakespeare's twenty or so triumphs—still rammed with life.

II

Jonson's magnificent vehemence carries him over to Volpone's side, in defiance of Jonsonian moral theory. Not that Volpone (and the plebeian Mosca even more so) is not hideously punished. He—like Mosca—is outrageously overpunished, which may be Jonson's self-punishment for the imaginative introjection of his greatest creation. Perhaps Jonson is chastising us also, knowing that we too would delight in Volpone. The representation of gusto, when worked with Jonson's power, becomes a gusto that captivates us, so that it scarcely matters if we remember how wicked Volpone is supposed to be. Massively aware of this paradox, distrusting the theatrical while creating Volpone as a genius of theatricality, Jonson takes moral revenge upon Volpone, the audience, and even himself. The imagination wishes to be indulged, and delights in being deceived. No playgoer or reader wishes to see Volpone's deceptions fail, and our delight is surely Jonson's delight also.

Robert M. Adams has some shrewd comments upon what I suppose we might want to call Jonson's ambivalences towards the theater:

> The tone of punishment and correction runs through a lot of Jonson's dramatic work; there are passages which don't come far short of suggesting that he thought the work itself a form of correction, if not punishment, for the audience: "physic of the mind" was one of his terms.

Jonson might have observed that he was following Aristotle's precepts, yet a "physic of the mind" does seem stronger than a catharsis. You tend to receive worse than you (badly) merit in Jonson, and that hardly purges you of fear. It is something of a mystery anyway why Jonson believed Volpone and Mosca needed to be so severely punished. Except for his exasperated attempt to rape Celia, Volpone preys only upon those who deserve to be fleeced, and thus defrauds only the fraudulent. Nor does Jonson represent Volpone's failed lust for Celia as being without its own imaginative opulence. As with Sir Epicure Mammon in *The Alchemist,* we hear in Volpone's mad eloquence the equivocal splendor of a depraved will corrupting imagination to its own purposes:

CELIA

> Some sérene blast me, or dire lightning strike
> This my offending face!

VOLPONE

>   Why droops my Celia?
> Thou hast, in place of a base husband, found
> A worthy lover: use thy fortune well,
>
> With secrecy and pleasure. See, behold,
> What thou art queen of; not in expectation,
> As I feed others: but possessed and crowned.
> See here a rope of pearl; and each, more orient
> Than that the brave Egyptian queen caroused:
> Dissolve and drink them. See, a carbuncle
> May put out both the eyes of our St. Mark;
> A diamond, would have bought Lollia Paulina,
> When she came in like star-light, hid with jewels,

That were the spoils of provinces; take these,
And wear, and lose them: yet remains an earring
To purchase them again, and this whole state.
A gem but worth a private patrimony,
Is nothing: we will eat such at a meal.
The heads of parrots, tongues of nightingales,
The brains of peacocks, and of ostriches,
Shall be our food: and, could we get the phoenix,
Though nature lost her kind, she were our dish.

CELIA

Good sir, these things might move a mind affected
With such delights; but I, whose innocence
Is all I can think wealthy, or worth th'enjoying,
And which, once lost, I have nought to lose beyond it,
Cannot be taken with these sensual baits:
If you have conscience—

VOLPONE

'Tis the beggar's virtue;
If thou hast wisdom, hear me, Celia.
Thy baths shall be the juice of gilly-flowers,
Spirit of roses, and of violets,
The milk of unicorns, and panthers' breath
Gathered in bags, and mixed with Cretan wines.
Our drink shall be preparéd gold and amber;
Which we will take, until my roof whirl around
With the vertigo: and my dwarf shall dance,
My eunich sing, my fool make up the antic,
Whilst we, in changèd shapes, act Ovid's tales,
Thou, like Europa now, and I like Jove,
Then I like Mars, and thou like Erycine:
So, of the rest, till we have quite run through,
And wearied all the fables of the gods.
Then will I have thee in more modern forms,
Attiréd like some sprightly dame of France,
Brave Tuscan lady, or proud Spanish beauty;
Sometimes, unto the Persian Sophy's wife,
Or the Grand Signor's mistress; and, for change,
To one of our most artful courtesans,
Or some quick Negro, or cold Russian;
And I will meet thee in as many shapes:
Where we may so transfuse our wandering souls
Out at our lips, and score up sums of pleasures.

It is difficult to believe that Jonson did not admire the superb audacity of Volpone's hyperboles, which out-Marlowe Marlowe. "Could we get the phoenix,/ Though nature lost her kind, she were our dish," is particularly fine, as that firebird, mythical and immortal, is always present only in one incarnation at any single moment. Heroic in the bravura of his lust, the Ovidian Volpone charms us by the delicious zeal with which he envisions Celia's changes of costume. Sir Epicure Mammon holds on always in my memory for his energetic "here's the rich Peru," but Volpone is positively endearing as he gets carried away in transports of voluptuousness, and bursts into strains of Catullus in his exuberance:

Come, my Celia, let us prove,
While we can, the sports of love,
Time will not be ours for ever,
He, at length, our good will sever;
Spend not then his gifts in vain:
Suns that set may rise again;
But if once we lose this light,
'Tis with us perpetual night.
Why should we defer our joys?
Fame and rumor are but toys.
Cannot we delude the eyes
Of a few poor household spies?
Or his easier ears beguile,
Thus removéd by our wile?—
'Tis no sin love's fruits to steal;
But the sweet thefts to reveal,
To be taken, to be seen,
These have crimes accounted been.

Jonas Barish, moved by his depth of Jonsonian scholarship to a Jonsonian moralizing, reads Volpone's Ovidian and Catullan allusions as evidence that: "Folly, vanity, lust, have been, are, will be. At any given moment their practioners are legion, and often interchangeable." Yes, and doubtless Jonson would have been gratified, but what about the verve, wit, lyric force, and intoxicating eloquence with which Jonson has endowed Volpone? Foolish and vain lusters may be interchangeable, but whom would you get if you gave up Volpone? We are again in the paradox of Jonson's theatrical art at its most extraordinary, which brings Volpone back to delight us after he has been so cruelly sentenced:

[VOLPONE comes forward]
The seasoning of a play is the applause.
Now, though the fox be punished by the laws,
He yet doth hope, there is no suffering due,
For any fact which he hath done 'gainst you;
If there be, censure him; here he doubtful stands:
If not, fare jovially, and clap your hands. [Exit]

THE END

Biography of
Ben Jonson

A few years after the peak of his dramatic career, Jonson ventured on a walking tour of Scotland. There he visited the poet William Drummond, whose notes on his conversations with Jonson comprise the basis for much of the current understanding of the writer's life. Drummond described Jonson as

> A great lover and praiser of himself; a contemner and scorner of others; given rather to lose a friend than a jest; jealous of every word and action of those about him, especially after drink (which is one of the elements in which he liveth); a dissembler of ill parts which reign in him, a bragger of some good that he wanteth; thinketh nothing well but what either he himself, or some of friends and countrymen, hath said or done. He is passionate kind and angry; careless either to gain or keep; vindictive, but if he be well answered, at himself.

It is impossible to assess the accuracy of this depiction, and there is ample evidence that Drummond and Jonson had divergent aesthetic tastes and incompatible personalities. Yet Drummond's estimation of Jonson as proud, jealous, and passionate man is supported by the record of his life.

Jonson was born in London in 1572, shortly after the death of his father, an Anglican minister. His mother remarried a bricklayer and, despite straitened circumstances, Jonson received substantial education. He attended the Westminster School, where he studied under the antiquarian William Camden, who remained a lifelong friend and teacher. Many of his peers went on to Oxford and Cambridge, but Jonson was apprenticed as a bricklayer. His apprenticeship was interrupted by military service in the Netherlands where Jonson challenged to combat and killed a Spanish soldier. It is unclear how long Jonson continued to work as a bricklayer, but in his conversations with Drummond, Jonson said that he 'could not endure' this profession, and certainly by the early nineties he had turned to other pursuits.

In 1594 he married Anne Lewis, whom he described to Drummond as "a shrew, yet honest." Jonson worked as an actor and writer for Philip Henslowe's theatrical company, The Admiral's Men, playing the lead role in Kyd's *Spanish Tragedy*. Jonson became an efficient writer, hastily producing many adapted works. Jonson did not include these plays in his collected works and *The Case Is Altered* (1597), is the only remaining example of this type of his drama. There are further gaps in our knowledge of Jonson's early writings; by 1598, Frances Meres listed Jonson in *Palladis Tamia* alongside Kyd and Shakespeare as one of the best writers of tragedy, yet none of the works that won him this recognition survived.

During this time, Jonson collaborated with Thomas Nashe on the satirical *Isle of Dogs*. Along with several other members of the company, Jonson was imprisoned because of "slanderous matter" in the play.

In 1598, *Every Man in His Humour*, Jonson's earliest successful play, and, by his own estimation, his first important drama, was performed by Lord Chamberlain's Men. Scholars have concluded that Shakespeare was part of the cast of *Every Man in His Humour* and also acted in the later tragedy, *Sejanus*.

During this year, Jonson killed the actor Gabriel Spencer in a duel. Though Jonson depicts a valiant portrait of himself in his account of the incident, claiming that Spencer attacked him with a sword ten inches longer than his own, Jonson pleaded guilty and was sentenced to be hanged. He saved himself only by claiming 'benefit of clergy,' a law that allowed literate, first-time offenders to escape death by reading a prescribed neck-verse. His possessions were confiscated and he was branded on his thumb as murderer. During his imprisonment a recusant priest visited him and Jonson subsequently converted to Catholicism.

Over the next three years, Jonson produced three comedies, *Every Man Out of His Humour* (1599), *Cynthia's Revels* (1600) and *Poetaster* (1601). Each of these satirical plays was part of the "War of the Theaters," an ongoing conflict, played out on the stage, between Jonson and contemporaries such as John Marston and Thomas Dekker. Because the insults incorporated into the plays increased the playwrights' commercial success, it is difficult to determine how much authentic animosity existed between them.

Despite these dramatic successes, Jonson did not rely entirely on his theatrical works for income. He benefited from private patronage, particularly after 1603 when James VI of Scotland, a supporter of the theater, came to power. Jonson then began a three decade career of writing court masques and entertainments.

Though Jonson continued to preside over a group of literary disciples that met at Mermaid Tavern, he suffered a difficult period. Following the disastrous failure of the tragedy *Sejanus*, Jonson suffered the loss of his son, killed at age seven by the plague. In 1604, Jonson collaborated with Marston and Chapman on the comedy *Eastward Ho!* The play satirized the Scots, and as the Scottish James VI was King at the time, Jonson was imprisoned. There were rumors that his ears and nose would be cut as punishment. Jonson was released without suffering this chastisement and celebrated his release in a banquet with friends. Drummond recorded that "at the midst of the feast, his old mother drank to him and shew (sic) him a paper which she had (if the sentence had taken execution) to have mixed in the prison among his drink, which was full of lusty strong poison; and that she was no churl, she told she minded first to have drunk it of herself."

With the success of *Volpone* (1605) Jonson began his period of comic maturity. *Epicoene* and *The Alchemist* followed in 1609 and 1610. In 1612, Jonson began working on a collective edition of his works and in 1615 Jonson produced his fourth great comedy, *Bartholomew Fair*. These successes were interrupted only by the failure of Jonson's return to tragedy, *Catiline* (1611). During this period, two women gave birth and recorded the father of the child as "Ben Jonson." Jonson gave up Catholicism in 1610 and reconverted to Anglicanism, drinking the entire chalice of wine at his first communion. In 1612, Jonson went to Paris and Brussels for a year as the tutor and governor to the son of Sir Walter Raleigh.

In 1616, *The Devil Is an Ass* was produced and the Folio Edition of his works completed. Including contemporary, commercial dramas in such a collection of literary works was an unprecedented, controversial move. In the following years his stature as an esteemed man of letters was firmly established. The King granted him a pension, an honor which came to be associated with the title of Poet Laureate and he received an honorary masters degree from Oxford.

However, Jonson was troubled by health and financial problems. Dependent on pensions from the King, the aging Jonson failed to win substantial support from Charles I. In 1623, a fire destroyed many of Jonson's writings in theology, philosophy, literary criticism and poetry. Five years later, he suffered a stroke, and he remained paralyzed and bed-ridden for the next nine years of his life, though he continued to write plays and poems. Probably due to his financial hardship, Jonson returned to the popular theater in 1629, with the catastrophic *The New Inn,* followed by the similarly disappointing *The Magnetic Lady* and *A Tale of a Tub.*

During the last years of his life, Jonson suffered considerable want. He died at Westminster, on August 6, 1637, at the age of sixty-five and was buried at Westminster abbey. No child of his survived him and his disciples became his literary executors. After his death, a volume of memorial tributes was published. Writers— poets, dramatists and critics—continue to acknowledge their debt to him. Poet and critic Algernon Charles Swinburne composed his tribute in the poem, *Ben Jonson,* which exquisitely captures the fiery, dark magic of Jonson's genius.

> Broad-based, broad-fronted, bounteous, multiform,
>   With many a valley impleached with ivy and vine,
> Wherein the springs of all the streams run wine,
>   And many a crag full-faced against the storm,
> The mountains where thy Muse's feet made warm
>   Those lawns that reveled with her dance divine
>   Shines yet with fire as it was wont to shine
> From tossing torches round the dance aswarm.

> Nor less, high-stationed on the grey grave heights,
> High-thoughted seers with heaven's heart-kindling lights
>   Hold converse: and the herd of meaner things
> Knows or by fiery scourge or fiery shaft
> When wrath on thy broad brows has risen, and laughed,
>   Darkening thy soul with shadow of thunderous wings. ❀

Plot Summary of
Every Man in His Humour

Every Man in His Humour was first presented in 1598, and first printed in a 1601 Quarto. A substantially revised version of the play was printed in the 1616 Folio edition of Jonson's works. Jonson made substantial changes to the drama, such as moving the setting from Italy to England. His revisions moved the play toward greater realism of human character and daily life in England.

Every Man in His Humour thus offers a unique perspective on Jonson's dramatic evolution and can be considered a product of two very different periods in his development. Critics have often analyzed the play by examining its adherence to and departures from classical rules. Many of the characters are loosely based on stock types, but Jonson has individualized them by his creative hand. More than they can be categorized by social type or class, the characters in the play are marked by their excessive "humour" or dominant passion. The play, in its revised form, is a celebration of the follies and errors of human life, which Jonson presents as the fruits of excessive humours. Pretense and social pretension are also central themes of the play, and it is not insignificant that nearly all forms of human folly presented in the play are exacerbated, if not caused, by hubris.

As the play opens, the cantankerous Old Kno'well laments his son's interest in the "fruitless and unprofitable art" (I.i.18) of poetry. Kno'well intercepts a letter of invitation from Master Wellbred to his son Edward, and, judging Wellbred to be a "profane and dissolute wretch," resolves to keep a close eye on his son. He instructs the servant Brainworm to give Edward the letter without revealing that he has opened it. In Scene Three, the young would-be poet Matthew seeks the braggart soldier Bobadill at the home of Cob, a witty water-bearer. Cob describes Matthew, a fishmonger's son, who attempts to "wriggle" his way into the acquaintance of young gentlemen, and spends his afternoons reading abominable poetry to ladies. Matthew complains to Bobadill that Downright openly mocked Matthew. An indignant Captain Bobadill vigorously urges Matthew to challenge Downright, and uses a bed staff to instruct the admiring Matthew on dueling techniques.

Act II begins in Kitely's home in the Old Jewry, as Kitely and Downright discuss their annoyance toward Wellbred, who makes Kitely's house a "public receptacle / For giddy humor," (II.i.57–8) gathering there with his "wild associates" (II.i.60) to "[s]wear, leap, drink, dance and revel" (II.i.62). As both his new wife and virgin sister reside in the house, Kitely reasons that if he voiced his objections, the other men would slander him as a jealous husband who evicted them out of a fear of being cuckolded. Kitely's subsequent speech describes his anxiety that with the "young revellers" his wife will not be honest long and demonstrates that he merely fears the gentlemen will suspect his honest fear. He goes on to describe the mechanism of his jealousy, exhibiting a high level of self awareness: "[I]t begins / Solely to work upon the fantasy. . . . As soon corrupts the judgment; and from thence / Sends like contagion to the memory. . . . spreads itself / Confusedly, through every sensitive part, / Till not a thought, or motion in the mind, / Be free from the black poison of suspect" (II.i.222–231). Despite this intellectual understanding of his passions, Kitely remains an utter slave to his fears.

Brainworm informs the audience that Kno'well has followed his son on his journey to visit Wellbred, and explains that he, siding with the young Edward, will disguise himself as a poor soldier and follow Kno'well. In his disguise, Brainworm gleefully gulls Edward and his dimwitted cousin Stephen, who, captivated with the project of becoming a valiant gentleman, foolishly purchases Brainworm's rapier. Brainworm then begs from Old Kno'well who is outraged that the soldier has so "sordid-base," and thus instructs Brainworm to follow him. Delighted with his jests, Brainworm jubilantly exclaims that he will observe Kno'well and share what he learns with Edward.

In Act III, Wellbred happily greets Edward at Windmill Tavern and Stephen and Matthew exchange self-important remarks about poetry and the art of being melancholy. Stephen shows off his new rapier, which, the group hastily informs him, is no rare Toledo but a common army issue. Brainworm arrives, reveals his identity to a delighted Edward, and informs him that Kno'well has followed him to the city.

Meanwhile, Kitely prepares to leave the house and begins to fret upon the risks of leaving his wife at home. Unable to overcome his doubts about trusting his servant Cash with his secret fear, Kitely simply tells Cash to send word if Wellbred returns to the house. The group returns and Cash dispatches Cob to inform Kitely of Wellbred's arrival.

In **Act IV**, Matthew recites plagiarized poetry to Bridget at Kitely's house, as the other young men watch in amusement. Downright grows increasingly infuriated with Wellbred and his friends and demands that they leave. The members of the household struggle to keep Downright from attacking the gentlemen, and Kitely returns to the chaos of their dispute. Bridget and Dame Kitely defend the visitors and Kitely interprets their comments as further proof that Dame Kitely is involved in an affair with Edward Kno'well. Echoing Kitely's jealousy, Cob instructs his wife to stay at home, allowing no one to enter, since she too may be tempted. Meanwhile, Edward shares with Wellbred his affection for Bridget.

At Edward's bidding, the disguised Brainworm tells Kno'well that Edward has discovered that his father is following him. Gulling Kno'well with a dramatic tale that Edward seized Brainworm and tried to force him to confess where Kno'well was, Brainworm incites Kno'well's fury against his son. Brainworm sends Kno'well to Cob's house, explaining that he will find his son meeting a married woman there. Meanwhile, the furious Downright attacks Bobadill, who cannot defend himself because Cob, after being beaten by Bobadill, has served him a warrant of the peace.

Brainworm returns to Kitely's house, disguised as Justice Clement's man, Formal. He distracts Kitely from the arrangements for the wedding of Edward Kno'well and Bridget, by falsely reporting that Clement desires to speak with Kitely immediately. Wellbred then gets rid of Dame Kitely, inciting her jealousy by suggesting that Kitely has gone to Cob's house to cheat on her. She sets out to pursue him. Kitely returns, and certain that Dame Kitely has left to cuckold him, goes to Cob's house in pursuit of her.

Bobadill and Matthew spot Formal (the disguised Brainworm) and request a warrant on Downright. Brainworm assures them he will provide it, delighting in his tricks.

The madness reaches its height in **Act IV**, Scene eight; at Cob's house, Kno'well demands that Tib produce his son. Dame Kitely arrives looking for her husband. When Kitely shows up she rails against him, but he answers her with accusations that she has come to Cob's house to sleep with Old Kno'well! When Kitely informs Cob that his wife is a running a brothel, he begins to beat her. Kno'well suspects that all this madness is part of a trick to justly "punish [his] impertinent search" for his son. The group resolves to have Justice Clement settle the matter.

Act V takes place at Justice Clement's house, where Clement slowly uncovers the true course of events. Brainworm reveals his identity and on the merit of his wit, the merry Clement pardons him for his devices. Clement has less mercy for the pretenders Bobadill and Matthew, the "sign of the soldier, and picture o' the poet," (V.i.247) and he sentences them to a penitent fast until midnight. Assured of her fidelity, Cob reconciles with Tib, as Clement resolves that Bridget and Kno'well will be married in the evening. Turning to the jealous pair of Dame and Mr. Kitely, Clement admonishes that "Horns i' the mind are worse than o' the head." Clement's call for all to join him in celebratory evening in honor of "friendship, love and laughter" closes the play. ❀

List of Characters in
Every Man in His Humour

Kno'well, an older gentleman, is the concerned father of Edward Kno'well. Throughout the drama he laments the younger generation's lack of decorum and he disdains his son's interest in poetry, recounting that he was once a student interested in such idle pursuits, but has since learned "to distinguish / The vain, from th'useful learnings" (I.i.22–3). Determined to keep a watchful eye on his son, Kno'well follows Edward to the city where Edward and Brainworm plot to gull him. At the close of the play, Edward forgives Kno'well for his well-meaning, but overbearing concern.

Edward Kno'well is an intelligent, cultured student who loves poetry. Edward develops affection for Bridget and Wellbred arranges a marriage between the two. Edward learns from his loyal servant Brainworm that his father has followed him to the city, and in response, employs Brainworm to gull his father.

Brainworm is the mischievous and jocose servant to Ed. Kno'well, who initiates the schemes that set the play's action in motion. Brainworm unequivocally sides with his young master, revealing to Edward that his father followed him and then artfully gulling Old Kno'well. Clement is so delighted by the genial sports of Brainworm that he pardons him at the end of the drama.

Master Stephen, cousin to Edward Kno'well is a dimwitted country gull whose fatuity is exacerbated when he finds himself a stranger in the city. Aspiring to be a gentleman of culture and valor, he admires Bobadill and buys a rapier from the disguised Brainworm. He fails to give an even mildly convincing performance that he is anything but a country fool and his inanity entertains Edward and Wellbred.

Downright, a choleric country squire and half-brother to Wellbred, is infuriated by Wellbred's disrespectful behavior and grows violent in his anger at Wellbred's circle of associates.

Wellbred is the witty young gallant who writes the provocative letter of invitation to Edward, causing Kno'well's alarm. He socializes with the group of young associates at Kitely's home. With Edward Kno'well, Wellbred takes amusement at the folly and stupidity of Stephen and Matthew.

Justice Clement is described by Wellbred as "a city magistrate, a justice . . . an excellent good lawyer, and a great scholar: but the only mad, merry fellow in Europe" (III.i.251–3)! He adores the play's witty deceivers like Brainworm and reproaches the weak pretenders such as Matthew. True to his name, Clement shows mercy to all at the close of the drama.

Thomas Kitely, a newly married merchant, is obsessed by fears that his wife is cuckolding him. Highly reflective about his all-consuming jealously, he is nearly unable to leave his sociable wife alone and employs his servant Cash to watch over her whenever he is away.

Master Matthew plays the role of melancholic poet and lover, reciting plagiarized verses of bad poetry throughout the play and attempting to woo Bridget. Cob describes the simple fishmonger's son, who "does . . . creep, and wriggle into acquaintance with all the brave gallants about the town" (I.iii.62–63). Like Stephen, Matthew admires Bobadill and attempts to imitate him, attentively listening to his instructions on fencing.

Oliver Cob is the simple but witty water–bearer, who becomes implicated in the confusion when his house is assumed to be the brothel which Edward Kno'well, Kitely and Dame Kitely use for their illicit rendezvous. When Kitely accuses Cob's wife Tib of being a bawd, Cob believes him and begins to beat her. He is reconciled to his wife at the close of the play.

Captain Bobadill is a belligerent braggart soldier, who endlessly discusses his military career, inspiring the admiration of Stephen and Matthew. Bobadill has genuine military accomplishments and a vast knowledge of warfare. ❀

Critical Views on
Every Man in His Humour

[Algernon Charles Swinburne (1837–1909) is best known
for his poetry but also composed brilliant essays of literary
criticism, many of which are collected in his *The Age of
Shakespeare* which covers numerous playwrights, including
Webster, Marston, Middleton and Marlowe. In this selection, Swinburne compares Jonson and Shakespeare and discusses Jonson's limitations, lack of spontaneity and his
encumbered verse.]

If poets may be divided into two exhaustive but not exclusive
classes,—the gods of harmony and creation, the giants of energy
and invention,—the supremacy of Shakespeare among the gods of
English verse is not more unquestionable than the supremacy of
Jonson among its giants. Shakespeare himself stands no higher
above Milton and Shelley than Jonson above Dryden and Byron.
Beside the towering figure of this Enceladus the stature of Dryden
seems but that of an ordinary man, the stature of Byron—who
indeed can only be classed among giants by a somewhat licentious
or audacious use of metaphor—seems little higher than a dwarf's.
Not even the ardour of his most fanatical worshippers, from the date
of Cartwright and Randolph to the date of Gilchrist and Gifford,
could exaggerate the actual greatness of his various and marvellous
energies. No giant ever came so near to the ranks of the gods: were it
possible for one not born a god to become divine by dint of ambition and devotion, this glory would have crowned the Titanic
labours of Ben Jonson. There is something heroic and magnificent
in his lifelong dedication of all his gifts and all his powers to the service of the art he had elected as the business of all his life and the
aim of all his aspiration. And the result also was magnificent: the
flowers of his growing have every quality but one which belongs to
the rarest and finest among flowers: they have colour, form, variety,
fertility, vigour: the one thing they want is fragrance. Once or twice
only in all his indefatigable career of toil and triumph did he achieve
what was easily and habitually accomplished by men otherwise

unworthy to be named in the same day with him; by men who would have avowed themselves unworthy to unloose the latchets of his shoes. That singing power which answers in verse to the odour of a blossom, to the colouring of a picture, to the flavour of a fruit,—that quality without which they may be good, commendable, admirable, but cannot be delightful,—was not, it should seem, a natural gift of this great writer's: hardly now and then could his industry attain to it by some exceptional touch of inspiration or of luck. ⟨. . .⟩ Reversing the famous axiom of Goldsmith's professional art-critic, we may say of Jonson's work in almost every instance that the picture would have been better if the artist had taken less pains. For in some cases at least he writes better as soon as he allows himself to write with ease—or at all events without elaborate ostentation of effort and demonstrative prodigality of toil. The unequalled breadth and depth of his reading could not but enrich as well as encumber his writings: those who could wish he had been less learned may be reminded how much we should certainly lose—how much of solid and precious metal—for the mere chance of a possible gain in spontaneity and ease; in qualities of lyrical or dramatic excellence which it is doubtful whether he had received from nature in any degree comparable with those to which his learning gave a fresh impulse and a double force of energetic life. And when his work is at its worst, when his faults are most flagrant, when his tediousness is most unendurable, it is not his learning that is to blame, for his learning is not even apparent. The obtrusion and accumulation of details and references, allusions and citations, which encumber the text and the margin of his first Roman tragedy with such a ponderous mass of illustrative superfluity, may undoubtedly be set down, if not to the discredit, at least to the disadvantage of the poet whose resolute caprice had impelled him to be author and commentator, dramatist and scholiast, at once: but however tedious a languid or a cursory reader may find this part of Jonson's work, he must, if not abnormally perverse in stupidity, admit that it is far less wearisome, less vexatious, less deplorable and insufferable, than the interminable deserts of dreary dialogue in which the affectations, pretentions, or idiocies of the period are subjected to the indefatigable and the lamentable industry of a caricaturist or a photographer.

There is nothing accidental in the work of Ben Jonson: no casual inspiration, no fortuitous impulse, ever guides or misguides his genius aright or astray. And this crowning and damning defect of a tedious and intolerable realism was even exceptionally wilful and premeditated. ⟨...⟩

—Algernon Charles Swinburne, *A Study of Ben Jonson* (London: Chatto & Windus, 1889): pp. 3–5, 7–9.

WILLIAM HAZLITT ON JONSON'S COMEDIES OF HUMOURS

[An eminent critic, journalist, and essayist, William Hazlitt (1778–1830) published several books of dramatic criticism, including the classic *Characters of Shakespear's Plays*. In this selection, Hazlitt compares Shakespear's comedies of character to Jonson's comedies of humours, as well as commenting generally on the strengths and weakness of the play.]

Every Man in his Humour, is a play well-known to the public. This play acts better than it reads. The pathos in the principal character, Kitely, is "as dry as the remainder biscuit after a voyage." There is, however, a certain good sense, discrimination, or logic of passion in the part, which affords excellent hints for an able actor, and which, if properly pointed, gives it considerable force on the stage. Bobadil is the only actually striking character in the play, and the real hero of the piece. His well-known proposal for the pacification of Europe, by killing some twenty of them, each his man a day, is as good as any other that has been suggested up to the present moment. His extravagant affectation, his blustering and cowardice, are an entertaining medley: and his final defeat and exposure, though exceedingly humorous, are the most affecting part of the story. Brainworm is a particularly dry and abstruse character. We neither know his business nor his motives: his plots are as intricate as they are useless, and as the ignorance of those he imposes upon is wonderful. This is the impression in reading it. Yet from the bustle and activity of this character on the stage, the changes of dress, the variety of affected tones and gipsy jargon, and the limping affected gestures, it is a very amusing theatrical exhibition. The rest, Master Matthew, Master Stephen, Cob and Cob's wife, were living in the sixteenth century. That is all we all know of them. But from the very oddity of their appearance and behaviour, they have a very droll and even picturesque effect when acted. It seems a revival of the dead. We believe in their existence when we see them. As an example of the power of the stage in giving reality and interest to what otherwise would be without it, I might mention the science in which Brainworm praises Master Stephen's leg. The folly here is insipid from its being seemingly carried to an excess, till we see it; and then we laugh the more at it, the more incredible we thought it before.

—William Hazlitt, *Lectures on the English Comic Writers* (New York: Russell & Russell, 1969): pp. 83–85.

ANNE BARTON ON JONSON'S REVISIONS TO THE PLAY

[Anne Barton is Professor at Trinity College, Cambridge. She is the author of numerous books on Shakespeare including, *Essays, Mainly Shakespearean* and *Shakespeare and the Idea of the Play*. She also authored *Ben Jonson, Dramatist* and *The Names of Comedy*. In this excerpt, Barton analyzes Jonson's changes to the Folio text of the play and demonstrates how these changes amend moments in the play when character and action are at odds with each other.]

When he revised *Every Man In His Humour,* after a lapse of years, and a series of experiments with comedies which had largely broken away from dependence upon a linear plot, Jonson recognized and tried to correct a number of misadjustments (as they now seemed to him) between the real substance of the play—including its characters—and its plot. The Folio text excises Thorello's last-minute harassment of Biancha, while adding the line which ensures recognition of the borrowed nature of his recantation. The effect is to maintain scepticism about the jealous man's conversion, but to make it less jarring in context. A similar intention seems to underlie the mitigated sentences passed on the characters now called Matthew and Bobadill. The Folio condemns them to nothing worse than a tedious and supperless wait in Clement's courtyard while the others are enjoying themselves inside. There is no attempt to bludgeon them into repentance—but no 'heroic' last statement by Bobadill either. Like his successor in *Every Man Out of His Humour*, Cavaliero Shift, Bobadill is silent after his pretensions have been finally exposed. These two changes help to make the last scene seem more balanced and at ease with itself, without pretending that 'such a one' can be turned into Sidney within twelve hours.

Jonson seems to have recognized and made attempts to amend a number of other rough places in the comedy where plot and its realization were at odds. He re-wrote Prospero's original letter to Lorenzo Junior in the country, making it more cheeky and irreverent, altogether more alarming reading for a fussy and overly protective father than the quarto version. This alteration acknowledges without really solving a problem. The letter still fails to motivate the elder Kno'well's anxiety in the tangible way that sons who have scandalously run off with flute girls, sunk themselves in all the sexual and financial iniquities of the town, or crossed their own father's plans for re-marriage can, and do, in Roman comedy. Like Lorenzo Senior in the quarto, old Kno'well still seems irrational when he hares off to the city in chase of a son whose behaviour gives no genuine cause for alarm and, even worse, sets up no definite objective on the level of plot which his father (or anyone else) can attempt to thwart.

> —Anne Barton, *Ben Jonson, Dramatist* (Cambridge: Cambridge University Press, 1984): pp. 51–52.

Simon Trussler on the Representation of Comic Character in the Play

[Simon Trussler is a retired drama professor at the University of London and the editor of *New Theatre Quarterly*. Trussler has edited and written the introductions for

[numerous recent editions of Marlowe's and Jonson's plays, and is the author of *The Cambridge Illustrated History of British Theater*. In this article, Trussler examines Jonson's non-individualized, "typically eccentric" characters and discusses how these figures create humor in the play.]

But whereas the conventional modern assumption suggests that it is the uniqueness of an individual's personal traits or temperamental make-up which makes him interesting, in life or art, this is arguably no more than leftover romanticism dignified by the 'science' of psychology. Whether following Aristotle or in blissful ignorance of his neo-classical apologists, pre-romantic artists were concerned rather with the task of portraying what was *typical*—and so universally true—in human nature. Thus, the popular Jacobean prose form of 'character writing' did not offer 'profiles' of individuals in the modern sense, but essayistic descriptions of types: the parson, the actor, the traveller, the hack poet, the dancer, the gull—or, at the level of more serious enquiry, the courtier, or the prince, whose qualities a Castiglione or a Machiavelli had earlier and so influentially tried to define.

It's important to stress this aim of 'typicality' in Jacobean writing, if only because Shakespeare (in Jonson's own tribute) made himself 'not of an age, but for all time' by so often departing from it. Jonson himself is often concerned less with typicality than with the 'typically' eccentric. But there's nothing unusual about this. It has been a method of comedy from Aristophanes to *The Young Ones* (the characters of which were duly berated by their visiting parents for not being in a 'nice' sitcom, such as respectable audiences have always preferred). Chaucer and the Wakefield Master knew about 'humours' technique, too: all Jonson did, with that flair for self-promotion he displayed throughout his life, was to find a catchy new label for an age-old way of making people laugh. ⟨. . .⟩

Bergson suggested that the source of laughter was rigidity—the inability of the mind to react with sufficient flexibility to a given situation: and that is arguably the clearest and funniest aspect of many of Jonson's characters. Shakespeare's 'comic' characters, on the other hand, tend to become less funny in inverse proportion to their complexity—or, if you like, to their flexibility. For Shakespeare, this is often tied up with matters of class: such laughter as there is derives from the low-life scenes of the sub-plots, or from a 'magical' rigidity imposed by disguise or the powers of faery. Jonson seldom condescends in this way. True to comic decorum, he does not often deal with the better classes of society: and his ordinary, middle- and working-class characters, whatever their faults, are what they are. In spite of the didactic intentions Jonson proclaimed in prologues, inductions and other critical bits-and-pieces such as Shakespeare assiduously refrained from writing, the people of his plays perkily transcend their supposed flaws and failures, to remain triumphantly or bathetically unchanged by their experiences.

—Simon Trussler, Commentary in *Every Man in His Humour* by Ben Jonson (London: Methuen, 1986): p. 13.

David Riggs on Jonson's Adaptation of Galen's Four Humours in the Play

[David Riggs is Professor of English at Stanford University. He specializes in Renaissance Literature and is the author of *Shakespeare's Heroical Histories: Henry VI and Its Literary Tradition* and the biography *Ben Jonson: A Life*. In this excerpt, Riggs discusses how Jonson draws upon and revises the Greek conception of the four humours, showing how it shapes both the characters and plot of the play.]

The originality of *Every Man in His Humour* lay in the claim to rigor and comprehensiveness implied by its title. Jonson's play does not merely recount a humorous day's mirth; it provides a general anatomy of human folly. Neoclassical critics, influenced by Aristotle's oft-cited pronouncement that comedy depicts men "worse than the average . . . not as regards any and every sort of fault, but only as regards one particular kind, the Ridiculous," were uniformly agreed that affectation and stupidity were the special province of the comic poet. Jonson accepted this dictum and all its implications. The comic poet was a supremely rational being—poised, aloof, indifferent to the vagaries of the marketplace—and his work portrayed precisely the opposite sort of person: nervous, self-absorbed, totally susceptible to the tug of novelty and fashion. Yet neoclassical theorists also emphasized that the butts of stage comedy should be *model* eccentrics, representative deviations from a norm that any educated person could recognize. On the face of it, this is a paradoxical proposition: what is meant by a "normal" oddity, or a "typical" curiosity?

In sorting out this puzzle, Jonson harked back to the older, medical sense of the word "humor," and discovered, in the psychology of the Galenic tradition, a coherent taxonomy of eccentric behavior patterns. The Greek physicians had originally conceived of the erring humors as a way of accounting for divergences from the ideal of perfect health. In a sound constitution, the four humors (bile, phlegm, choler, and blood) are perfectly blended and, hence, untraceable. When a humor transgresses its proper boundaries, however, it generates systemic disruptions. ⟨. . .⟩

Galen divided the spectrum of human eccentricity into four humors, but Jonson adopted the simpler, and equally commonplace, bipolar scheme based on psychological disorders associated with choler and blood. While choler manifests itself in excessive anger, the sanguine humor, if carried to extremes, can lead to incontinent or perverted sexual desire. These two stereotypical obsessions, which correspond to the irascible and concupiscent temperaments, are the foundation of Jonson's comedy of humors. On a purely verbal level, they are personified by Captain Bobadilla, the braggart warrior, and Matheo, the plagiarizing love poet. ⟨. . .⟩

Just as Galen's semiotics furnished Jonson with a complete set of character types, Galen's pathology supplied the basic outline of his comic plot. When a humor enters a state of flux, it encroaches upon the neighboring organs, which then absorb the humor, grow distended, and either burst or—if the outcome is successful—reject it. The physicians refer to this process as "coction"—a kind of slow, physiological cooking. Once the body has expelled the indigestible waste products that cannot be assimilated into a wholesome organism the erring humors return to a state of equilibrium. The same principles apply to the working out of a comic narrative. Jonson assembles a variety of characters who exhibit symptoms of the humoral disorders. They overflow into houses and rooms that are too constricted to contain them ⟨. . .⟩. Thrust into the streets, the humors abandon their normal family ties and merge into fluid syndicates of irate and erotic types. The humors feed on delusions of grandeur, but all their victories are Pyrrhic, for the bigger a disorder becomes, the harder it is to satisfy. Having outgrown the limits of domestic order, they recklessly transgress the limits of civil rule and their collapse follows swiftly and inevitably. As the distempered humors die of their own excess, their healthy counterparts (Prospero, Young Lorenzo, and Hesperida) compose themselves into a new and harmonious mixture. The braggart warrior and the plagiarizing sonneteer are analogous to the unwholesome remnants that the body rejects during the final stage of the therapeutic process: when Doctor Clement formally expels them from the concluding feast, the cure is complete.

—David Riggs, *Ben Jonson: A Life* (Cambridge, Massachusetts: Harvard University Press, 1989): pp. 38–41.

ROBERT N. WATSON ON NATURALISM IN THE PLAY

[Robert N. Watson served as Chair of the Department of English at UCLA and as Chair of the Faculty of the UCLA College of Letters and Science. He is the editor of *Critical Essays on Ben Jonson* and of the New Mermaids edition of Jonson's *Every Man in His Humour.* He authored *Shakespeare and the Hazards of Ambition, Ben Jonson's Parodic Strategy: Literary Imperialism in the Comedies,* and *The Rest Is Silence: Death as Annihilation in the English Renaissance.* In his analysis, Watson emphasizes the naturalistic aspects of the drama, focusing on human pretense and role-playing as a central theme.]

Every Man In is innovative comedy precisely because it is business as usual. The roadside negotiations between Stephen and Brainworm over the sword may be outdated in their commodity and coinage, but not at all in their character: the hustling salesman passes off his inferior product as the fancy imported kind, flattering the buyer's judgement and asking him merely to offer a fair price, while the buyer, after hollowly demanding the salesman's lowest price, ends up buying the product more for pride and self-image than for any real need. Jonson's London may have been, as many scholars claim, a society rapidly and radically shifting from an archaic feudal system toward modern capitalism, but this transaction is as old as Plautus, and as recent as your last shopping trip.

So while Jonson may—proudly—deny us the romantic transcendences of Shakespearean comedy, he does offer a revelation of transhistorical human tendencies, as they manifested themselves at a specific historical moment, which encouraged role-playing in the cause of social-climbing. ⟨. . .⟩

Editors of Jonson's 'humours' plays feel obliged to explicate the Renaissance medical taxonomy that associated character traits with an imbalance among bodily fluids (one producing anger, another melancholy, and so on). But Jonson's use of the term is unorthodox. Distinguished early critics of the play such as William Congreve set the tone by defining a humour as a man's unique and unchangeable self, yet closer study suggests that it is virtually the opposite: a conventional fictional disguise the self chooses, which is by no means his own, and often the opposite of his true nature. Though the play bears some structural analogies to a humoural cure, Jonson's characters are driven less by chemistry than by fantasy; they are less what they eat than what they read. After all, Bobadill only pretends to be belligerent, and Matthew only pretends to be a melancholic lover. The idea that Jonson conceives the humours which control human action as essentially verbal rather than physical—not the fluids of one's body but the language of one's fluency—fits nicely with the evidence that he conceived the theatre and even the soul as more verbal than physical. His suggestion that 'Painting and carpentry are the soul of masque' in the 'Expostulation with Inigo Jones' is bitterly sarcastic. Language is power: because he can talk like a soldier and like a lawyer, Brainworm easily takes Old Knowell's secrets, Formal's clothing, Downright's and Stephen's money, finally even Downright's and Stephen's bodies into custody.

So if these victims seem like stock characters, it may be because they are 'humouring' themselves, selling to themselves or to the world a formulaic idea of their natures and their status, mediated by words. All Stephen's efforts—practising 'the hawking and hunting languages', for example—are directed towards being called a 'gentleman'. Bobadill's swordsmanship is all talk (plus a little mathematics), and when Stephen wants to become Bobadill, he simply emulates his oaths. When Matthew wants to prove himself romantically melancholy, he plagiarizes love-poetry. Even Cob tries to pun his way into a royal lineage. Kitely admits to having learned his final speech 'out of a jealous man's part in a play'. This pattern, greatly magnified in the revision of the play, allows Jonson to attack his literary rivals (a favourite occupation) because many of the characters are trying to play conventional dramatic roles of the period, which Jonson subjugates to the 'realities' of his own London scenes.

—Robert N. Watson, Introduction to *Every Man in His Humour*, by Ben Jonson (London: A & C Black, 1998): pp. xi–xiv.

Plot Summary of
Volpone

Considered Jonson's first masterpiece, *Volpone* has been highly praised since its initial performance. A comedy, *Volpone* portrays dark plots and evil motives that are fit for tragedy, though Jonson's characters could not sustain tragic treatment. Mosca and Volpone craft the deception of the greedy gulls around them like playwrights and actors intoxicated by their creations.

Volpone confesses in the **opening scene** that he "glor[ies] / More in the cunning purchase of [his] wealth" (I.i.30–31) than in his riches. What then, does Volpone seek? His unnamed obsession remains ambiguous, but as witnesses to his vitality, wit and eloquent speech, attentive readers cannot fail to sense that he seeks more than gold and sport. When Volpone is punished at the end of the play, that within the reader that applauded his audacity and imagination suffers great indignation and can hardly believe that Jonson felt his Volpone met a fitting end.

The drama opens as Volpone joyously praises his riches, speaking about his gold as if it was a God, describing how he "shrine[s]" (I.i.2) his wealth and reveres it as "the world's soul and [his own]" (I.i.3). He explains that he plays with the hopes of "women and men of every sex and age" (I.ii.77) who compete for his inheritance.

Volpone assumes his disguise as ailing patient and Mosca, his obsequious servant, gleefully laughs about the gulling that will occur. In each of the following three scenes, a greedy hopeful visits and is tricked by clever Mosca.

The lawyer Voltore, "the vulture" presents Volpone with an antique plate, as Mosca shrewdly manipulates Voltore's hopes, assuring him that he is the sole heir. Next, aged Corbaccio, the "raven," an "impotent" "wretch" (I.iv.3) arrives. Mosca suggests that, to demonstrate his love for Volpone, Corbaccio disinherit his son and make Volpone his heir. Corbaccio's greed, as well as Mosca's manipulation, is the grounds for his gulling: Corbaccio agrees to the plan, claiming it was his own idea. Soon Corvino, "the kite," arrives, offering Volpone jewels as Mosca pledges that Corvino will inherit the riches.

Volpone, delighted with Mosca's brilliant gulling, calls for "music, dances, banquets all delights" (I.v.87). As the act closes, Mosca mentions Corvino's beautiful wife, inspiring Volpone's desire to see her. Because she is "kept as warily as gold" (I.v.19) by Corvino, they resolve to go in disguise to her window.

Act II opens with a comic exchange between the pretentious fool, Sir Politic Would-Be, a knight and English traveler, and Peregrine, a gentleman traveler whom he meets in the street. Sir Politic enthusiastically tells Peregrine the English "news," mentioning various events that he foolishly interprets as omens. Peregrine humors Sir Politic and sarcastically praises his vast knowledge.

Disguised as the mountebank Scoto Mantuano, Volpone stands under Celia's window, delivering long-winded speeches about his merchandise. He announces that the first person to toss their handkerchief will receive a "little remembrance" (II.ii.207). Celia throws hers and Volpone presents her with a beautifying powder. An irate Corvino enters and beats Volpone away.

Volpone desperately tells Mosca that Cupid "hath shot himself into [him] like a flame" (II.iv.6) and Mosca schemes to help Volpone achieve his desire. Meanwhile, an incensed Corvino rages at Celia for interacting with "a prating mountebank" (II.v.2). Having devised his plan, Mosca informs Corvino that Volpone's health can only be preserved if a young woman, "Lusty, and full of juice . . . sleep by him" (II.vi.35). When Mosca notes that a physician volunteered his virgin daughter, Corvino offers Celia.

Act III opens as Mosca delights in his own cunning. Mosca tells Bonario that Corbaccio has disinherited him and invites the incredulous son to witness his father's deed. Meanwhile, Lady Would-Be garrulously converses with Volpone, whose sarcastic asides serve as a comic refrain to her chatter. To get rid of her, Mosca informs Lady Would-Be that he saw Sir Politic with a courtesan and she promptly departs to pursue him.

Mosca hides Bonario, but the plan goes awry when Corvino, not Corbaccio, arrives at the house. Mosca and Corbaccio leave Celia with Volpone, who makes a curious attempt to woo her, singing a love song, offering his riches, and reciting his fantasies of their "sports of love." Her pious refusal is resolute, and Volpone begins to forcibly take her. But Bonario leaps out from his hiding place, rescuing Celia and fleeing with her. Volpone's desperate cry, "Oh! I am unmasked, unspirited, undone . . ." (III.vii.277–8) concludes the scene.

Mosca offers Volpone his repentant sorrow and soon Mosca is again at work with his deft trickery. Mosca informs Corbaccio that Bonario somehow learned that he was disinherited, and entered Volpone's house in an attempt to kill his father. Appalled at his son's intentions, Corbaccio gives Mosca the will declaring Volpone his heir. Mosca then artfully explains to Voltore that he is working a plot on Voltore's behalf: Corbaccio will leave his fortune to Volpone; Mosca will incite Bonario to murder his father, and, as Volpone's heir, Voltore will inherit twice the riches. Mosca then crafts another lie, saying that at the house Bonario seized Celia, and forced her to affirm that Volpone had raped her. Voltore is utterly gulled by Mosca's lies.

Act IV's opening scene offers a welcome diversion from Mosca's dark plots. Sir Politic Would-Be offers Peregrine absurd advice about decorum in Venice. Sir Politic's comic paranoia leads him to see everything as a devious plot devised against him. This is deliberately juxtaposed with the naiveté of Volpone's victims, who, in the midst of plots, suspect nothing. With great earnestness, Politic shares with Peregrine the secret projects he is planning. The hilarity increases when Lady Would-Be assumes Peregrine to be the disguised whore accompanying her husband. Moments later, Mosca informs her that Sir Politic's courtesan has been apprehended. The "blushing" Lady Would-Be begs Peregrine's pardon.

Mosca's gulling grows more complex; he has devised a plan for what Corvino, Corbaccio and Voltore will say in court, and clandestinely assures each that he is working to ensure their inheritance. Having heard Celia and Bonario's testimonies, the Avvocati marvel at the immoral acts of Corvino and Corbaccio. As Mosca instructed him, Voltore declares that Bonario and Celia have been engaged in an adulterous affair. He continues with Mosca's version of the story, which defames the lovers and emancipates Volpone and the suitors from all culpability. Lady Would-Be enters, and with Mosca's prompting, adds to their case, crying out that Celia is the "harlot" she saw with her husband.

When Volpone enters, the Avvocati's judgment is fully swayed. Appearing frail and hardly able to move, he is no likely rapist. The

Avvocati have Celia and Bonario seized and Volpone, "the old gentleman" returned to his home. Mosca goes back to his sport and adds another player to his game, informing Lady Would-Be that he will attempt to persuade Volpone to put her in his will.

At the opening of **Act V**, Volpone's morale is fading, but he gives himself wine for cheer and to revive himself with further gulling, resolves to "vex" the hopefuls. He sends Nano and Castrone to announce that he is dead. When three suitors arrive, hidden Volpone watches with glee as they realize that Mosca is his heir. Yet Volpone craves further amusement, and Mosca resolves to steal a commendatore's uniform so that Volpone may harass them outside in disguise.

As Volpone and Mosca gratuitously mock Voltore, Corvino and Corbaccio, a disguised Peregrine, tricking Sir Politic, tells Politic that Peregrine was a spy who has reported to the Senate Politic's scheme "to sell the state of Venice to the Turk" (V.iv.38). Terrified that he will be arrested, Sir Politic hides in a Tortoise shell, and a farcical scene follows. When Politic is thoroughly humiliated, Peregrine reveals himself and Politic resolves to return to England!

Scene five is a crucial turning point in the play. Mosca turns against Volpone, deciding to lay a "Fox-trap," and asserting, "I'll bury him or gain by him. I'm his heir . . ." (V.v.4). In the street, the disguised Volpone mocks the misfortunes of Corvino, Voltore and Corbaccio.

Provoked by this derision, Voltore begins to confess the truth to the court. Volpone regrets his folly, as he needlessly mocked Voltore, causing himself further trouble with the law. Volpone suspects that Mosca has betrayed him, and at the court, his suspicions are confirmed. Mosca fails to affirm the disguised Volpone's claims, and the Avvocati have him taken away.

Reasoning that a confession can't cause anything worse than his impending imprisonment, Volpone reveals his identity. Yet, this is faulty reasoning; Volpone's confession suggests that after Mosca's betrayal, he has little left to live for.

The true course of events becomes clear to the Avvocati, who grant Bonario and Celia their liberty, and sentence the others to punishments fitting their crimes: Mosca will be imprisoned for life. Volpone will be kept in a hospital where he will be "cramped with irons" until he is as lame and sick as he had feigned. Voltore is banished from the law; Corbaccio is sent to a monastery, and Corvino is ordered to be rowed around Venice wearing ass's ears, and must send his wife home to her father. Volpone closes the play, asking the audience for applause. ❀

List of Characters in
Volpone

Volpone, the Fox, is an eloquent, charismatic figure, whose speech brings to the play its most impressive poetry. Volpone loves to play-act, and relishes his performances as the infirm patient, taking equal pleasure in his roles of Scoto Mantuano and the commendatore. He is in fact a wealthy, elderly, childless man, whose heirless fortune attracts "new clients, daily to [his] house" (I.i.76) bringing gifts and feigning love. Often thrilled by his and Mosca's gulling, Volpone derives greater delight from theatrical sports than by his riches.

Mosca, Volpone's sycophantic servant, uses his persuasive speech and insightful understanding to carefully manipulate the gulls, maintaining their hopes, extorting gifts and all the while convincing each that he is their dutiful advocate and best ally. If Volpone is a kind of actor, Mosca is his cunning director and often his playwright. In Act III, giddy with delight at his outrageous successes, Mosca deems himself a true parasite: ". . . your fine, elegant rascal, that can rise / And stoop (almost together) like an arrow; / Turn short, as doth a swallow; and be here, / And there, and here, and yonder, all at once; / And change a visor swifter than a thought (III.i.23–9)!

Voltore, a lawyer, vies to be Volpone's heir. Unlike Corbaccio and Corvino, Voltore perpetrates no familial betrayals in pursuit of the riches. Following Mosca's plan, Voltore presents an extensive, articulate argument against Bonario and Celia at the court. He is the first to be panged by conscience, and confesses his own dishonesty to the Avvocati. Hopelessly blinded by his own greedy hopes, Voltore is yet again gulled by Volpone, and recants his confession. He is ultimately banned from the law by the Avvocati.

Corbaccio, an elderly gentleman, hopes to be Volpone's heir. Near death himself, he is mocked throughout the play for his old age and poor hearing. Attempting to poison Volpone during his visit in Act I, he repeatedly suggests that Mosca kill his master. The extent of Corbaccio's greed is made clear when he tells Mosca that he too thought about disinheriting his son in order to ingratiate himself to Volpone. At the close of the play, the Avvocati give his estate to Bonario and send him to a monastery.

Corvino, violent and controlling husband to Celia, commits the most egregious evil of the three greedy gulls. Irrationally jealous of his pious wife, Corvino threatens to physically torture Celia and later, adhering to Mosca's plan, slanders his wife in court to prevent his own shameful deed from being revealed. At the close of the drama, the Avvocati order that Corvino send Celia home to her father and return her dowry. He is also sentenced to being rowed around Venice "wearing a cap with fair long ass's ears" (V.xii.137).

Avvocati are the four magistrates of the court, who repeatedly change their position as they successively hear conflicting testimonies regarding Volpone in Acts IV and V of the play. When the true villains of the situation are clearly revealed, they dole out fitting punishments for each of the offenders, carefully crafted to respond to the criminals' temperamental flaws as well as their particular crimes.

Nano, the dwarf, lives with Volpone. With Castrone and Androgino, he entertains Volpone and Mosca with games and merriment. In the poem he recites for Volpone's amusement in Act III, Nano describes himself as the "little," "witty," and "pretty" (III.iii.9–10) creature who imitates men's actions "in a ridiculous fashion" (III.iii.14).

Castrone, the eunuch, entertains Volpone and Mosca, singing a song in praise of fools to Volpone in Act I.

Sir Politic Would-Be, is an earnest, fatuous, English knight and tourist in Venice. Volpone's subplot, essentially comprised of the antics and exploits of Sir Politic Would-Be and his wife, offers crucial comic-relief from the central story. Though forthcoming and sociable, Politic is convinced that dark plots and political intrigue surround him. His schemes and humiliation by Peregrine are of a fundamentally different order than the plots and trickery of Mosca, Volpone and their gulls.

Peregrine, a sensible gentleman-traveler, derives great amusement from Sir Politic Would-Be's ridiculous advice for travelers and nonsensical schemes for improving the state of Venice. Peregrine disguises himself, gulling and humiliating Sir Politic Would-Be.

Bonario, son of Corbaccio, is disinherited by his father who, in the hopes of inheriting Volpone's fortune, makes Volpone his legal heir. When Volpone attempts to rape Celia, Bonario reveals himself, protects her as the two escape, and reports this wrongdoing at the court. A victim of his father's greed, Bonario continually protests throughout the court scenes, and like Celia, is a voice of morality in the play.

Fine Lady Would-Be, wife to Sir Politic is a garrulous Englishwoman constantly displaying her interests in Italian culture and poetry. Fussy, socially ambitious, and endlessly chatty, Lady Would-Be possesses a strong appetite for interpersonal drama and, like her husband, often appears absurd because of her obvious misperception of her own importance.

Celia, wife to Corvino, is an emblem of innocence and piety in the play. Volpone is captivated by her beauty and with Mosca, devises a plan by which he will enjoy her. Prizing her honor above all else, Celia entreats first Corvino and then Volpone to kill her rather than destroy her purity. Celia pleads and prays throughout the trial, where she is accused of being a duplicitous harlot. When the men are captured, she interjects a brief plea for the Avvocati to treat them mercifully.

Androgino, the hermaphrodite, lives with and entertains Volpone and Mosca. He wittily jests with Nano in a dialogue about the transmigrations of his souls in Act I. ❀

Critical Views on
Volpone

C. H. HERFORD AND PERCY SIMPSON ON VOLPONE AS
COMEDY APPROACHING TRAGEDY

[Herford (1853–1931) and Simpson are co-editors of the
exhaustive Oxford *Ben Jonson*. C. H. Herford, Litt.D.,
Trinity College, is Professor of English Literature in the
University of Manchester. He is the author of *Shakespeare
and the Arts; Shakespeare; Wordsworth; Robert Browning;
The Permanent Power of English Poetry;* and *A Sketch of
Recent Shakespearean Investigation, 1892–1923*. Percy
Simpson is author of *Studies in Elizabethan Drama, The
Theme of Revenge in Elizabethan Tragedies, Proof-Reading in
the 16th, 17th and 18th Centuries,* and *Biographical Study of
Shakespeare*. In this selection, they discuss the ways in which
the play is influenced by and approaches tragedy, noting
departures from comic conventions in both the action of
the play and the drama's characters.]

With *Volpone* Jonson returned, in his own view at least, to comedy.
But it was to comedy widely different from all previous work of his
own in that kind, and rather hard to accommodate not merely to the
elastic Elizabethan notions of comic art, but (what Jonson cared
much more for) to 'the strict rigour of' ancient '*comick* law'. In the
sternness of the catastrophe, as Jonson felt, it approached tragedy.
And in its whole conception and conduct, in the lurid atmosphere
which pervades it from beginning to end, in the appalling and menacing character of the principal movers of the plot, it approaches,
not indeed the profound and human-hearted tragedies of Shakespeare, but, very obviously and significantly, his own grandiose and
terrible tragedy of two years before. ⟨. . .⟩

If *Volpone* marks a wide departure from the realism he had earlier
enjoined upon the comic dramatist, it violates still more strikingly
his second demand, that comedy should 'sport with human follies',
not with 'crimes'. If Jonson ever 'sports' here, it is in the sombre and
lurid fashion of his own 'sporting Kyd'. There is folly enough, to be
sure; but it is the formidable and menacing folly of men who have
capacity and resource and absolutely no scruples, and whether such

men commit follies or crimes is merely a question of occasion and circumstance. All the principal persons are capable of any crime; they are gamblers playing desperately for high stakes, and when they see their advantage, Corbaccio plays his son's inheritance, and Corvino his wife's honour. The moral repulsion, however, with which they so powerfully affect us is less due to the actual crimes and vices they perpetrate than to the impression of unlimited possibilities of evil which they convey. 〈. . .〉

The three dupes are drawn in less detail but with a no less incisive and powerful hand. They stand clearly and unmistakably apart, but not because they differ a jot in the quality or degree of their rapacity. Raven, crow, vulture, they represent but a narrow class even among birds of prey. They differ in their circumstances, not in their bent. Voltore, the knowing advocate, is as blinded by greed and as easily gulled as the dull and deaf Corbaccio, and executes volte-faces when the cause requires it as shamefully as Corvino. Wonderfully as the adventures of the three are invented and discriminated, one cannot but contrast with the unrelieved monotone of their decadent and criminal corruption the picturesque diversity of the clients of Subtle and Face. Both the strong ethical bias which animated Jonson in *Volpone,* and the comparative absence of realistic stimulus and suggestion, contributed to this effect. In no other of the comedies are the persons so sharply distinguished as bad or good. The rank and uniform depravity of the rogues and dupes is set off by the white innocence of Celia and Bonario, who to tell the truth are, as characters, almost as insipid as they are innocent. Even the *avocatori* fall apart into two corresponding groups,—the three abstract and colourless administrators of justice, and the 'fourth', who seeks to temper its rigour to a possible son-in-law. Of the proper and normal material of comedy, extravagancies and absurdities, there is, in the main plot, nothing. Its nearest approach to humour lies in the horrible simulations of the ludicrous effected by the misshapen creatures of Volpone's household.

—C. H. Herford and Percy Simpson, *Ben Jonson: Volumes I & II, The Man and His Work, The Second Volume* (London: Oxford University Press, 1925): pp. 49–50, 55, 63–64.

BEN JONSON ON THE MORAL IMPORT OF THE PLAY

[Benjamin Jonson was an English Jacobean dramatist, poet, and literary critic. Regarded as the second most important English dramatist, after William Shakespeare, Jonson was esteemed as a erudite man of letters and gifted playwright. His major plays include the comedies *Every Man in His Humour* (1598), *Volpone* (1605), *The Alchemist* (1610), and *Bartholomew Fair* (1614). In this excerpt, Jonson discusses the didactic and moral aspects of his play.]

For if men will impartially, and not asquint, look toward the offices and function of a poet, they will easily conclude to themselves the impossibility of any man's being the good poet, without first being a good man. He that is said to be able to inform young men to all good disciplines, inflame grown men to all great virtues, keep old men in their best and supreme state, or, as they decline to childhood, recover them to their first strength; that comes forth the interpreter and arbiter of nature, a teacher of things divine, no less than human, a master in manners; and can alone, or with a few, effect the business of mankind—this, I take him, is no subject for pride and ignorance to exercise their railing rhetoric upon. But it will here be hastily answered that the writers of these days are other things; that not only their manners but their natures are inverted, and nothing remaining with them of the dignity of poet but the abused name, which every scribe usurps; that now, especially in dramatic, or—as they term it—stage poetry, nothing but ribaldry, profanation, blasphemy, all licence of offence to God and man, is practised. ⟨. . .⟩

⟨I⟩n this my latest work (which you, most learned arbitresses, have seen, judged, and, to my crown, approved), wherein I have laboured, for their instruction and amendment, to reduce not only the ancient forms, but manners of the scene: the easiness, the propriety, the innocence, and last the doctrine, which is the principal end of poesy, to inform men in the best reason of living. And though my catastrophe may, in the strict rigour of comic law, meet with censure, as turning back to my promise; I desire the learned and charitable critic to have so much faith in me, to think it was done of industry. For with what ease I could have varied it nearer his scale, but that I fear to boast my own faculty, I could here insert. But my special aim being to put the snaffle in their mouths, that cry out we never punish vice in our interludes, &c., I took the more liberty; though not without some lines of example drawn even in the ancients themselves, the goings-out of whose comedies are not always joyful, but oft-times the bawds, the servants, the rivals, yea, and the masters are mulcted. And fitly, it being the office of a comic poet to imitate justice and instruct to life, as well as purity of language, or stir up gentle affections. To which I shall take the occasion elsewhere to speak.

—Ben Jonson, *Dedicatory Epistle* from "Volpone" in *Ben Jonson: Selected Works,* ed. Harry Levin (New York: Random House, 1938): pp. 959, 962.

ALVIN B. KERNAN ON THE SIGNIFICANCE OF VOLPONE'S ACT AS SCOTO MANTUANO

[Alvin B. Kernan has served as Professor of English at Yale and Princeton and is a senior advisor in the humanities at the Andrew W. Mellon Foundation. He is the author of numerous books of literary criticism, including *Shakespeare, The King's Playwright in the Stuart Court, 1603–1613; Death of Literature; Modern Satire;* and *Two Renaissance Mythmakers: Christopher Marlowe and Ben Jonson.* He has also authored an academic memoir, *In Plato's Cave* and *Crossing the Line,* a highly praised memoir of his naval service in World War II. In this excerpt, Kernan closely examines Volpone's speeches as Scoto Mantuano, arguing that they explore both Volpone's character and the therapeutic purposes of Jonson's comedy.]

In Act II, Scene 2 of *Volpone,* Volpone, in order to gain a sight of the pure Celia, whom he desires, assumes the mask of a mountebank, Scoto of Mantua, and delivers a long harangue on the virtues of his medicinal oil. Aside from its slight function in the plot, the speech serves to characterize Volpone and suggest his unlimited confidence in himself, his joy in skilfully playing a part, his delight in words, and his pleasure in bilking the ignorant clods of the world. ⟨. . .⟩

But there appears to be still another level of meaning in the mountebank's long spiel. At one point in his diversified entertainment, Volpone has his attendants sing the following song:

You that would last long, list to my song,
Make no more coyle, but buy of this oyle.
Would you be ever faire? and yong?
Stout of teeth? and strong of tongue?
Tart of palat? quick of eare?
Sharpe of sight? of nostrill cleare?
Moist of hand? and light of foot?
(Or I will come neerer to't)
Would you live free from all diseases?
Doe the act, your mistris pleases;
Yet fright all aches from your bones?
Here's a med'cine, for the nones.

                                        (II.2.192–203)

Most immediately the song is, of course, typical of the attitudes
Volpone represents in his own person, for we are offered here only
physical well-being, and this freedom from the pains that flesh is
heir to is offered on the impossible terms of perpetuity. But read in
a metaphorical rather than a literal fashion, the song suggests the
sanative goal of the satirist, the return to health of the individual
and society through the curative properties of satire itself. Quickness of ear, sharpness of sight, clearness of nostril would correspond on this level to moral rather than sensual alertness, an
ability to see, hear, and smell the moral foulness of the greedy, self-
centered, and unnatural men and women presented in *Volpone*.
Finally, and most importantly, the "oil" would restore man to his
procreative functions and allow him to reproduce his kind, to give
life and beauty to the world, rather than the misshapen creatures,
the dwarf, hermaphrodite, and eunuch, produced by Volpone. In
terms of this metaphorical interpretation of the song—and the
scene of which it is a part—the mountebank's nostrum or oil
would be Jonson's satiric plays, and the mountebank would
become Jonson the satiric poet.

  Certain details of the speech suggest this interpretation, for at
times the language of the mountebank gives way entirely to the language of a poet defending the peculiar value of his own satiric plays.
For example, the mountebank attacks "these ground *Ciarlitani,* that
spread their clokes on the pavement, as if they meant to do feates of
activitie, and then come in, lamely, with their mouldy tales out of
Boccacio" (II.2.49–51). And he goes on to inveigh against these same
rogues who "with one poore groats worth of unprepar'd antimony,
finely wrapt up in severall *'scartoccios* [papers], are able, very well, to

kill their twentie a weeke, and *play*." But, the mountebank goes on, "these meagre starv'd spirits . . . want not their favourers among your shrivel'd sallad-eating *artizans*." This poet-mountebank sounds very like the Ben Jonson who under many guises in the various prologues and epilogues of his plays praised the soundness of his own inventions, their decorousness and moral purpose, and berated the sensational, imitative, formless, and stale, but unfortunately popular and profitable plays of his contemporaries. ⟨. . .⟩

The mountebank's speech makes it clear, if my reading is correct, that while Jonson's methods of constructing satiric drama have changed, his aims have not. Under cover of the medical metaphor, so typical in satire, the satiric author now offers his play as a purge for the ills of the time. The medicinal properties of his product are no longer concentrated in the railing speeches of a satyr satirist but are present in the entire spectacle he places before us. The material out of which the mountebank compounds his medicinal oil and the materials out of which Jonson the satiric poet constructs *Volpone* are one and the same.

—Alvin B. Kernan, *The Cankered Muse* (New Haven: Yale University Press, 1959): pp. 164–168.

Una Mary Ellis-Fermor on Jonson's Affection Toward the Character Volpone

[Una Mary Ellis-Fermor was lecturer in English literature, Bedford College, University of London. She served as the General Editor of the New Arden Shakespeare and authored *Frontiers of Drama; Christopher Marlowe; Jacobean Drama: An Interpretation;* and *Shakespeare the Dramatist.* In this selection she discusses the playwright's special relationship to the figure of Volpone, arguing that Jonson created a uniquely exuberant character for whom he had unmatched feeling and affection.]

⟨. . .⟩ In *Volpone*, that masterpiece so sublimely simple and homogeneous in its mood of purposed evil, the compact flawlessness of the first four acts is only equalled or surpassed in Jonson's age by his own two succeeding comedies. Moreover, in this play there stirs something that we hardly meet else in Ben Jonson's writings, the promise, continually upon the verge of fulfilment, of that passionate obsession in the author with the figure of his own creating that is familiar to us in nearly all of his contemporaries: in Webster, Dekker, Chapman, Marston, Beaumont and Fletcher, Shakespeare himself and Ford, and is utterly alien to Ben Jonson's detached moralist's art. Ever and again about the figure of Volpone there moves, undefinable and unseizable, this sense of an imagination kindling not to critical denunciation, but to oblivion of critical positions, to identifying of itself with the passion and the power of its own creation. It is impossible to Ben Jonson wholly to allow this, since Volpone was originally begotten of his moral satire, but equally impossible wholly to impoverish him, to strip away a certain magnificence of daring, the high insolence with which, unaware, he has himself fallen in love. When, in the fifth act, the moment comes for the reversal and unmasking of this figure, when like Subtle or Morose he should have been driven into ignominious terms, we realize suddenly what hold this magnificent insolence has laid upon Jonson's imagination. For at the last moment Volpone revolts and, like an equally potent and equally rebellious creation of Shakespeare's, nearly wrecks the play. Mosca (and perhaps Ben Jonson himself) realizes too late that it is no slave-minded craven whom he is blackmailing, but an aristocrat whose high spirit he has failed to gauge. With one last terrific gesture, utterly unbefitting a comedy and all but precipitating it into tragedy, Volpone pulls down disaster upon himself and his enemy alike. 'I limmed this night-piece and it was my best'; the pride of Lodovico himself dictates his last free gesture and he withdraws, no way disabled in mind or spirit, a Venetian magnifico still. Never again did Jonson come so near feeling for a character of his own creating an admiration like that he gave to the two great contemporaries whom he reverenced, and the closing scenes of *Volpone* are his comment on the Jacobean ideal of an aristocrat, his characteristic variant of the theme 'I am Duchess of Malfi still'.

Indeed, paradoxically, almost perversely, from the opening lines of Volpone's slow-moving monologue, it is the splendour of the play that haunts us, a splendour that is symbolized superficially by the gold and massive plate of the legacy-hunters and finds its antitype in the depths below depths of evil into which the characters coldly and resolutely plunge. Cruel and ruthless as they are, repulsive and contemptible as they are all intended to appear, the very solidity of the atmosphere of evil lends, as in the otherwise dissimilar *Revenger's Tragedy,* and *Changeling,* a greatness to their tenacity and their resolution. By a supreme act of imagination Ben Jonson has penetrated behind the melodramatic semblances with which tradition had invested the Machiavellian plotter and exposed the cold concentration, the flawless courage which was a major quality—if not the major quality—of the portrait Machiavelli drew. Small wonder then that for posterity this play rivals even *The Alchemist* and, for some of us, seems the supreme reach of Ben Jonson's poetic power.

—Una Ellis-Fermor, The Jacobean Drama: An Interpretation (New York: Vintage Books, 1964): pp. 113–114.

LEO SALINGAR ON THE MOTIVATIONS BEHIND VOLPONE'S TRICKS

[Leo Salingar was a fellow of Trinity College, Cambridge. He is the author of *Shakespeare and the Traditions of Comedy* and "Comic Form in Ben Jonson: Volpone and the Philosopher's Stone." In this excerpt, Salingar analyzes Volpone's interactions with Celia and argues that Volpone's real interest is not in riches but in a rejuvenative life-force.]

⟨. . .⟩ The sense that Volpone pursues an elixir, or believes he already possesses an equally magical secret, is all the more potent in the play because his obsession is not directly named. Not to say what he is after is part of his mystification; and, if anything, he thinks of himself as a Machiavellian, rather than a vulgar adept (part of the effect of Sir Pol's role in the comedy is to throw light on this kind of self-deception among the Venetians). But Volpone is an adept in spite of himself. As soon as his imagination has been inflamed by the mere description of Celia, the course he takes to see her is to disguise himself as a mountebank, with a 'precious liquor' for sale. ⟨. . .⟩

And, once he has caught Celia's attention from her window, he tries to hold it with praise of an even rarer secret, his powder—⟨. . .⟩

Volpone here is acting, but acting with conviction; he is not trying simply to deceive the ignorant crowd, but to make an impression on the woman he intends to seduce. His rhapsody of perpetual 'life' is an ironic sequel to his diagnosis of Corbaccio.

Similarly, when he tries to seduce Celia, it is the dream of sexual vigour perpetually renewed that animates him, as he throws off his disguise of decrepit age:

> I am, now, as fresh,
> As hot, as high, and in as jovial plight,
> As when (in that so celebrated *scene*,
> At recitation of our *comœdie*,
> For entertainement of the great VALOYS)
> I acted yong ANTINOUS.
>
> (II.vii.157)

A Jacobean spectator, struck by that precise reference, could have reflected that the role had been hardly flattering to the actor's virility, and that the famous 'entertainement' was some thirty years back. In any case, the present Volpone must be old enough for the rumour of his physical decay to be believed. Yet what riles him, when Celia holds him off, is the horror reflected in his own lucrative pretence:

> Thinke me cold,
> Frosen, and impotent, and so report me?
> That I had NESTOR's *hernia*, thou wouldst thinke.
>
> (III.vii.260)

It is significant that the turning-point of the play should come here, in a scene of attempted rape, and not in an episode of fraud. References to health, medicine, disease, images connected with the life-force, are even more insistent than thoughts and images connected with money. And with an exact sense of the appropriate, Jonson has Volpone sentenced at the end, not for obtaining money under false pretences, but for simulating disease:

> our judgement on thee
> Is, that thy substance all be straight confiscate
> To the hospitall, of the *Incurabili*:
> And, since the most was gotten by imposture,
> By faining lame, gout, palsey, and such diseases,
> Thou art to lie in prison, crampt with irons,
> Till thou bee'st sicke, and lame indeed.
>
> (V.xii.118)

Volpone has been 'by bloud, and ranke a gentleman', stooping to a beggar's cony-catching tricks. But his essential crime has been an offence against Nature. ⟨...⟩

⟨...⟩ Materially speaking, the magnifico does not need to go in for fraud. He does it for his private 'glory', to 'cocker up [his] *genius*'; he feels a compulsion towards play-acting, preferably with a strain of the abnormal or the exotic. He needs spectators, but secret spectators whom he governs, including 'the curious' and 'the envious', whom he imagines spying on his love-making with Celia (III.vii.236–9). Above all, he needs to act a part, to the accompaniment of his own applause. A man of mature age, he feigns senility. As a would-be love-adventurer, he mimics a charlatan. Having recalled, to impress Celia, an image of himself as a youthful actor, he tries to dazzle her, beyond the pitch of '*vertigo*', with the prospect of making love 'in changed shapes', copied from Ovid's *Metamorphoses* and then furnished from a collector's wardrobe of exotic 'moderne formes' (III.vii.219, 221–55). Finally, escaping, thanks to Mosca, from the fear of exposure, his immediate recoil is to look for 'Any device, now, of rare, ingenious knavery, / That would possesse me with a violent laughter' (V.i.14), so that he brings retribution down on himself by way of his superfluous disguise as an officer of the law. Jonson has calculated Volpone's assumed roles so as to reflect back on his real personality; or rather, to reflect back on a being with a compulsive ego but no firm identity, a man perpetually 'forgetfull of himselfe' and 'in travaile with expression of another'.

—Leo Salingar, *Dramatic Form in Shakespeare and the Jacobeans* (Cambridge: Cambridge University Press, 1986): pp. 165–168.

JONAS A. BARISH ON THE SIR POLITIC AND LADY WOULD-BE SUBPLOT

[Jonas A. Barish is Professor of English at the University of California at Berkeley. He is the author of *The Antithetical Prejudice* and *Ben Jonson and the Language of Prose Comedy*. In this excerpt, Barish argues for the relevance of Volpone's subplot, analyzing the way Lady Would-Be and Sir Politic

Would-Be echo and mimic the action of the central characters of the play.]

For more than two centuries literary critics have been satisfied to dismiss the subplot of *Volpone* as irrelevant and discordant, because of its lack of overt connection with the main plot. Jonson's most sympathetic admirers have been unable to account for the presence of Sir Politic Would-be, Lady Would-be, and Peregrine any more satisfactorily than by styling them a "makeweight" or a kind of comic relief to offset the "sustained gloom" of the chief action. Without questioning the orthodox opinion that the links of intrigue between the two plots are frail, one may nevertheless protest against a view of drama which criticizes a play exclusively in terms of physical action. What appears peripheral on the level of intrigue may conceal other kinds of relevance. And it is on the thematic level that the presence of the Would-be's can be justified and their peculiar antics related to the major motifs of the play.

John D. Rea, in his edition of *Volpone,* seems to have been the first to notice that Sir Politic Would-be, like the characters of the main plot, has his niche in the common beast fable: he is Sir Pol, the chattering poll parrot, and his wife is a deadlier specimen of the same species. Rea's accurate insistence on the loquaciousness of the parrot, however, must be supplemented by recalling that parrots not only habitually chatter, they mimic. This banal but important little item of bird lore offers a thread whereby we may find our way through the complex thematic structure of the play. For Sir Politic and Lady Would-be function to a large extent precisely as mimics. They imitate their environment, and without knowing it they travesty the actions of the main characters. In so doing, they perform the function of burlesque traditional to comic subplots in English drama, and they make possible the added density and complexity of vision to which the device of the burlesque subplot lends itself.

His effort to Italianize himself takes the form, with Sir Politic, of an obsession with plots, secrets of state, and Machiavellian intrigue. His wife, on the other hand, apes the local styles in dress and cosmetics, reads the Italian poets, and tries to rival the lascivious Venetians in their own game of seduction.

Further, and more specifically, however, Sir Politic and Lady Would-be caricature the actors of the main plot. Sir Pol figures as a comic distortion of Volpone. As his name implies, he is the would-be politician, the speculator *manqué,* the unsuccessful enterpriser. Volpone, by contrast, is the real politician, the successful enterpriser, whose every stratagem succeeds almost beyond expectation. Sir Pol, like Volpone, is infatuated with his own ingenuity, and like Volpone he nurses his get-rich-quick schemes; but none of these ever progresses beyond the talking stage. While Volpone continues to load his coffers with the treasures that pour in from his dupes, Sir Pol continues to haggle over vegetables in the market and to annotate the purchase of toothpicks.

Lady Would-be, for her part, joins the dizzy game of legacy-hunting. Her antics caricature the more sinister gestures of Corvino, Voltore, and Corbaccio. She is jealous, like Corvino, as meaninglessly and perversely erudite as Voltore, and like Corbaccio, she makes compromising proposals to Mosca which leave her at the mercy of his blackmail. But, like her husband, Lady Would-be is incapable of doing anything to the purpose, and when she plays into Mosca's hands in the fourth act, she becomes the most egregious of the dupes because she is the blindest.

—Jonas A. Barish, "The Double Plot in *Volpone*" in *Ben Jonson,* ed. Harold Bloom (New York: Chelsea House Publishers, 1987): pp. 9–10.

WILLIAM EMPSON ON VOLPONE'S FALL

[Eminent poet and critic William Empson (1906–1984) taught English literature at the University of Tokyo, later joined the English faculty of Peking National University in China and became professor of English literature at Sheffield University in 1953. His main critical works include *Seven Types of Ambiguity, Some Versions of Pastoral; The Structure of Complex Words;* and *Milton's God.* In this selection, Empson discusses Mosca's betrayal of Volpone and discusses the significance of Volpone's broken-hearted response.]

Mosca seems an undeveloped character, but this is not a fault of the author, nor yet an illustration of a profound theory that all characters ought to be undeveloped. One might indeed complain that one or two of Mosca's comments are too magnificent to belong to him:

> Bountiful bones! What horrid strange offence
> Did he commit 'gainst nature, in his youth,
> Worthy this age?

(that is, making him deserve to become this horrible old man); but such rhetoric can be viewed as simply imitated from his master, for whose feelings he has a real sympathy; also, it helps to keep up a uniformity of tone. Apart from that, the plot requires Mosca to be a conventional-minded parasite, actually *trying* to be a "typical" one, because this is what causes his downfall. At the start of act 3, the correct point for the "crisis" of the design, he tells us what a clever parasite he is, and we find at once that he has overplayed his hand. He planted the good young man as a witness to something else, but events move too fast, and now the witness knows that Volpone is not dying. Disaster is only averted by the splendid impudence of Mosca at the trial, aided by the contemptible behaviour of the misers; but the nerve of Volpone is shaken by having to appear in court, and this causes his fatal error, which begins act 5. After being carried home, he looks round for a yet more reckless action, to recover his nerve:

> 'Fore God, my left leg 'gan to have the cramp,
> And I apprehended straight some power had struck me
> With a dead palsy. Well, I must be merry

—or fear will give him a disease; so he drinks, and as usual on the stage the effect is immediate:

> Tis almost gone, already; I shall conquer.
> Any device now, of a rare ingenious knavery
> That would possess me with a violent laughter
> Would make me up again.

That is, not only his chief pleasure, but his basic confidence, his assurance that his view of the scene around him is correct, comes from being able to fool in a spectacular manner these great world bankers, so as to prove that he completely understands their folly. It is plain here that Jonson was not still operating on the crude theory about "humours" which he had used earlier while struggling and frustrated. Unless you accept Volpone as an unusual character, almost as complicated as those of Shakespeare which the same audience enjoyed, the story is merely incredible. Be this as it may, after Volpone and Mosca have boasted together a little, tenderly though Mosca rallies him a bit to calm his fears, he signs a will leaving Mosca his entire fortune and tells Mosca to announce that he is dead. It is done with no expectation of further gain, merely to torment the expectant misers and induce them to act still more absurdly. Mosca comes to feel uneasy about this, after dismissing three misers with insults one after another, while he works away at his accounts and Volpone (like the author as usual) peers delightedly from the wings; Mosca suspects that they may feel too insulted to continue the arrangement after the truth becomes known; but Volpone feels certain that they will swallow any insult to get his fortune. ⟨. . .⟩

⟨Volpone⟩ is handing Mosca the ideal situation to betray him (exposing a servant to temptation, as my mother used to say). Indeed, Mosca might claim later to have only protected Volpone's interests by refusing to recognise him. But Mosca seems to look at him as a chess player might do at an opponent who is sacrificing his queen: "Did you really mean to do that? Well, I must take the obvious advantage, whatever you have in mind"; so he captures the queen. At first he only demands half, but when Volpone rejects this with indignation he becomes absorbed in the fun of trickery and conflict—he has no idea that he is breaking Volpone's heart, or at least exasperating the pride which in a Venetian grandee is even more dangerous. In the final trial, he orders Volpone the supposed policeman to be whipped for insolence to himself, now in Volpone's place; perhaps he feels that the extravagance of the presumption makes him safe, because no one could suspect he is doing it. Jonson is careful not to let the farce become weepy at the climax, and Volpone merely asks the audience to agree with him that "if I confess, it cannot be much worse"; but it is, and the real reason why he chooses to confess is that he has nothing left to live for, and would prefer to be wronged under his own high name. ⟨. . .⟩

—William Empson, "Volpone" in *Ben Jonson's* Volpone, or the Fox, ed. Harold Bloom (New York: Chelsea House Publishers, 1988): pp. 22–25.

Plot Summary of
The Alchemist

The Alchemist is likely the most popular of Jonson's plays. Critics have lauded the drama as a superbly constructed comedy that offers ingenious characters with widely diverse personalities. The play takes place within a house of mischievous cozenry where greedy gulls are tricked, humiliated, and cheated out of their money. *The Alchemist* truly comes alive when one imagines this house as a world of its own, as real as Jonson's words are vibrant. With Face as its God and Subtle as its Governor, this world has its own rules and exists only during the finite period when Lovewit is away.

Though at first they seem like mere greedy fools, each of the gulls who visits the house longs for a kind of transformation of self, and enters hoping to actualize their dreams. Intoxicated by their hopes, these gulls willingly delude themselves and ignore every visual and logical sign that they are being cheated, allowing Face's powerful rhetoric to persuade them. As the philosopher's stone transforms base metals into gold, the cozeners create a world of magic and hope as well as deceit and disappointments with their potent, creative language.

The play opens with an explosive argument between Face and Subtle, who exchange scathing insults as Doll attempts to quell their fighting. Through this squabble, one learns that while his master was away, the housekeeper Face set up the penniless cozener Subtle in his master's house, providing him with props and customers for his tricks. Doll also participates in their gulling, often playing the bawd. Lovewit, Master of the house, will return at a near, unknown date. The promise of his impending return alters the import of the gulling; the spectator is always aware that the mischief will come to an end and be somehow accounted for.

As the introductory scene closes, the games of gulling which drive the play's action begin. The lawyer's clerk Dapper arrives seeking supernatural improvements to his gambling luck. As Dapper's advocate to the learned "Doctor" (Subtle disguised in Doctor's robes), "Captain Face" manipulates the gambler's hopes and his purse with persuasive rhetoric. Subtle tells him that he is "allied to the Queen of Faery," and sends him away to prepare for a meeting with the Queen.

The tobacconist Drugger arrives, seeking mystical counsel on how to arrange his store. Subtle appears as an astrologer, offering ample advice as Face again duplicitously acts as the victim's advocate while cozening him out of his money.

Their next visitor is Sir Epicure Mammon, who has commissioned Subtle to make the "philosopher's stone," which transforms base metals into gold. Face appears as Lungs, assistant to Subtle, now disguised as a humble, pious Alchemist. Mammon's verbose speeches about the stone as rejuvenative and curative panacea are interrupted by the terse, sarcastic replies of his skeptical companion Surly, whom Mammon persistently ignores.

Face and Subtle devise a trap that will serve to explain the eventual absence of the stone: Doll sexually entices Mammon, and Face, pretending to be his victim's ally, offers to arrange a secret meeting between them. He warns Mammon that the stone will be ruined if the pious Alchemist discovers their licentious rendezvous. He also informs Mammon that Doll is a religious scholar driven mad who suffers loud fits whenever religion is mentioned. Meanwhile, skeptical Surly plots to catch the cheaters.

The cozeners are visited by Ananias, a member of the extreme Puritan sect of Anabaptists, who are mocked as corrupt hypocrites throughout the play. In the hopes of increasing their power, the Anabaptists have commissioned the Alchemist to produce the stone. After Ananias departs to tell his superior that further funds are needed to complete the project, Drugger arrives, requesting advice on the name of his shop. He mentions a young, rich, widow, Dame Pliant, who desires to have her fortune read and her brother Kestrel, who wishes to learn "quarreling." Face and Subtle urge Drugger to bring them to the house, and hoping to make the most of their contact with Pliant, draw straws to determine who will attempt to marry her. From this first discussion, Pliant inspires a tense rivalry between the two cozeners.

In **Act III**, the action accelerates as the gulling, once carefully controlled by Face, rapidly devolves into the cozeners' desperate efforts to prevent their duplicity from being exposed. Ananias returns with his superior Tribulation, who is easily seduced by Subtle. As they depart, Face turns to a new gull, a Spanish Count who seeks a prostitute. Face instructs Doll to seduce the count, but Dapper arrives, eager for his meeting with the Queen. Moments later, Drugger shows up with Kestrel. These coinciding visits upset the cozeners' plans and Face scrambles to keep up their charade.

Face enchants Kestrel with reports of Subtle's skills, and convinces Kestrel to bring his sister to the house. The cozeners then turn to the farcical humiliation of the Dapper, blindfolding him and confiscating his jewelry and money, explaining he cannot carry worldly possessions when meeting the Queen. Their elaborate performance is interrupted by Mammon's arrival and they lock Dapper in the toilet, assuring him the Queen will see him shortly. They soon forget him as they attend to the growing chaos in the house.

To Face's great amusement, Mammon delivers elaborate speeches of flattery in his attempt to woo Doll, whom he thinks is a scholar and a lady. Kestrel returns with Dame Pliant, and Face and Subtle's anxious competition over Dame Pliant continues to intensify. They reaffirm that they will draw straws to determine fairly who will win her. As Face and Subtle frantically try to keep their visitors in separate parts of the house, the Count arrives. Problematically, Doll's services are required for the gulling of Dapper, and the Count, so Face and Subtle cannot proceed until she is finished with Mammon.

Believing that the Count cannot speak English, Face and Subtle speak openly of their cozenry. The Count is in fact the disguised Surly, who understands every word. Adamant that they provide the count with a woman, Face plots to make Dame Pliant act as the Count's whore.

Face begins persuading Dame Pliant to marry a Spanish Count. He is aided by Kestrel who, gulled by Face, threatens to beat his sister should she refuse. Subtle then tells Dame Pliant that Spanish custom requires women to make the first amorous advances. Pliant departs with the Count, and Face cues Doll to feign her fit. Subtle, acting as the appalled, pious Alchemist, unleashes his fury on Mammon, and Face informs Mammon that his lust has destroyed the stone. With shame and regret, the disconsolate Mammon departs.

Though this scheme has succeeded, moments later Surly reveals his identity to Dame Pliant and confronts the cozeners. Surly's accusations, however, are no match for Face's art and he is forced out of the house, as Face persuades Drugger, Ananias and Kestrel that Surly is a jealous defamer.

The riotous gulling comes to a sudden stop when Doll announces that Lovewit has returned. He stands outside the house, assaulted by neighbors' accounts of what has transpired while he was away. But Lovewit, true to his name, is delighted and exclaims, "I love a teeming wit, as I love my nourishment" (V.i.16).

Appearing as Jeremy the butler, Face stammers in a weak attempt to explain the neighbor's remarks, as if he lost his talent for impromptu deceptions when he abandoned his disguise. When Dapper's cry suddenly bursts forth, Lovewit demands the truth from Face, who, at this moment, changes his tactic. Betraying Doll and Subtle, Face makes a new compact with his master, admitting to his crimes, but ingratiating himself to Lovewit by promising his master the hand of Dame Pliant.

Telling Subtle that Lovewit suspects nothing, Face orchestrates Dapper's meeting with the Queen. Subtle, believing that Face schemes to marry Dame Pliant, plots with Doll to cheat Face out of their jointly won riches. However, when the three gather again, Face abruptly announces that he has betrayed them, explaining that Lovewit has forgiven him and will keep their riches. Face offers them the choice of escape out the back, or confront the officers at the door. Doll and Subtle flee over the back wall, leaving with nothing of the cozened riches.

In the **final scene**, a smug Lovewit appears in the costume of a Spanish count, having wed Dame Pliant, as the furious gulls continue to pound on the door outside. Lovewit dismisses the officers, explaining that he rented his house to a corrupt Doctor for whose actions he is not responsible. Exhibiting his own cunning, Lovewit deftly gets rid of Mammon, Surly and the Anabaptists and Kestrel. In their concluding speeches Face and Lovewit address the audience. Departing from the convention of requesting the audience's applause, each apologetically acknowledges their failures and eccentricities, as if Jonson is aware that only after such a disclaimer could the audience respond to this ambiguous, troubling ending with happy applause. ❁

List of Characters in
The Alchemist

Subtle, allegedly a practitioner of the alchemical arts, is in fact a scheming front man for Face's plots. Though he does not possess the native cunning that Face brings to their cozenry, Subtle has sufficient knowledge of alchemy, astrology, and other necromantic arts to deceive the pair's victims. He poses as a doctor to Dapper, an astrologer to Drugger, and as a pious, humble alchemist to Mammon. Eventually betrayed by Face in Act V, Subtle escapes with Doll and most likely returns to the impoverished life he led before encountering the crafty butler.

Face, the housekeeper, is the mastermind behind the tricks and games of the venture tripartite of Subtle, Doll and himself. He is in fact the butler Jeremy, who, while his master was away, picked up the destitute Subtle and arranged for him to cheat willing gulls in his master's house. Face brings the gulls to Subtle, artfully acts as if he is their advocate, and manipulates them into giving up their money. Face remains a calculating trickster to the end, protecting himself by turning on his partnership and gulling in the service of his master Lovewit.

Doll Common, first introduced as she attempts to calm the argument between Subtle and Face, is part of their "venture tripartite" but never succumbs to the kind of petty disagreement, mutual suspicion or rivalry which exists between Face and Subtle. She most often plays the role of bawd, and her importance to the cozening is underscored by the need for her to be simultaneously present to Mammon as the mad scholar, Dapper as Queen of Faery, and the Spanish Count as prostitute. A sensible, pragmatic, and good-humored cozener, Doll, like Subtle, is cheated by Face at the end of the play.

Dapper, a lawyer's clerk, seeks Subtle's assistance to improve his luck at gambling, but is gulled into believing that he is "allied" to the Queen of Faery, a lone, rich woman who may bequeath her wealth to him. Locked in the toilet when Mammon's gulling takes precedence over his own, Dapper emerges in Act V, prompting Lovewit to demand the truth from Face.

Abel Drugger, a simple tobacco-man, arrives seeking mystical counsel on where to place the doors, shelves and other items in his shop so that his business will thrive. Later he returns seeking a lucky name for his shop. Utterly gulled by Face, Drugger becomes a useful help to him, referring to him Dame Pliant and Kestrel, defending Face against Surly's accusations and fetching Face a Spanish costume to aid the housekeeper's plots.

Lovewit, master of the house, is a cunning, intelligent, and self-satisfied man whose embrace of Face's mischief brings the play to a surprising, complex close. He returns from his travels in Act V of the play, forgives Face and quickly becomes a schemer and plotter with him. He deceives the officers and poses as the Spanish Count in order to marry Dame Pliant.

Sir Epicure Mammon, a knight, is the principal gulling project of the three cozeners, and by many scholars' estimations, one of Jonson's most impressive creations in this drama. He commissions the Alchemist to produce the philosopher's stone. The dreamer Mammon needs little assistance from Face as he easily becomes enraptured by his own high aspirations. Mammon's elaborate fantasies about the stone and the effusive speeches he employs in an attempt to "woo" Doll, constitute some of the finest comic and poetic moments in the drama.

Pertinax Surly, a gamester, is the skeptical and sarcastic companion to Mammon who declares upon his first visit to the alchemist that he will not be gulled. Unwavering in his contempt towards the cozeners, Surly tries, unsuccessfully, to reveal their duplicity to Mammon. To catch them, he disguises himself as a gullible Spanish Count who speaks no English, and thereby witnesses their cozening and lies. Jonson rewards neither his skepticism or his nobility; he is defeated by the accusations of the other gulls and he saves Dame Pliant's honor, only to lose his opportunity to marry her by doing so.

Tribulation Wholesome, a pastor of Amsterdam, concurs with Ananias' assertion that the Alchemist is a profane person but argues that the Anabaptists must "bend unto all means" no matter how impious, to "give furtherance to the holy cause" (III.i.11–12). Groveling and apologizing to the Alchemist for Ananias' contemptuous remarks, Tribulation is so fooled by the Alchemist that he eventually begins to believe, at Subtle's suggestion, that counterfeiting money for his brethren in Holland is legal.

Ananias, Anabaptist deacon of Amsterdam, is a unique figure among the gulls because he has doubts, not of the Alchemist's credibility, but about his moral stature. He voices these concerns patently throughout the play, arousing the feigned indignation of Subtle and the embarrassment of the pastor Tribulation, who wholeheartedly supports the Alchemist.

Kestrel, brother to Dame Pliant, is referred to Subtle by Drugger. He arrives to learn the art of quarreling and Face easily persuades him that the Doctor is an expert in this and many other arts. His interest in quarreling inspires many comic moments in the play: Face shrewdly seizes upon Surly's attacks on the cozeners as a moment for Kestrel to practice his art, thereby preoccupying Kestrel and simultaneously using him to defeat Surly. Kestrel's ignorance leads him to force his sister to marry the Spanish Count, as he is gulled by Face's ludicrous promises about the wealth she will enjoy as a countess.

Dame Pliant, a nineteen year-old rich widow and sister to Kestrel, is the mutual object of Subtle's and Face's desire and the cause of the jealous conflict between them. Jonson creates almost no personality for her, but Pliant is significant as Subtle's and Face's interest in her fuels much of the plot. ❀

Critical Views on
The Alchemist

ALGERNON CHARLES SWINBURNE'S COMPARISON OF *THE ALCHEMIST* AND *VOLPONE*

[Algernon Charles Swinburne (1837–1909) is best known for his poetry but also composed brilliant essays of literary criticism, many of which are collected in his *The Age of Shakespeare* which covers numerous playwrights, including Webster, Marston, Middleton and Marlowe. In this excerpt, Swinburne compares plot and character representation in *Volpone* and *The Alchemist*.]

In 1605 the singular and magnificent coalition of powers which served to build up the composite genius of Jonson displayed in a single masterpiece the consummate and crowning result of its marvellous energies. No other of even his very greatest works is at once so admirable and so enjoyable. The construction or composition of *The Alchemist* is perhaps more wonderful in the perfection and combination of cumulative detail, in triumphant simplicity of process and impeccable felicity of result: but there is in *Volpone* a touch of something like imagination, a savour of something like romance, which gives a higher tone to the style and a deeper interest to the action. The chief agents are indeed what Mr. Carlyle would have called 'unspeakably unexemplary mortals': but the serious fervour and passionate intensity of their resolute and resourceful wickedness give somewhat of a lurid and distorted dignity to the display of their doings and sufferings, which is wanting to the less gigantic and heroic villainies of Subtle, Dol, and Face. The absolutely unqualified and unrelieved rascality of every agent in the later comedy—unless an exception should be made in favour of the unfortunate though enterprising Surly—is another note of inferiority; a mark of comparative baseness in the dramatic metal. In *Volpone* the tone of villainy and the tone of virtue are alike higher. Celia is a harmless lady, if a too submissive consort; Bonario is an honourable gentlemen, if too dutiful a son. The Puritan and shopkeeping scoundrels who are swindled by Face and plundered by Lovewit are viler if less villainous figures than the rapacious victims of Volpone.

As to the respective rank or comparative excellence of these two triumphant and transcendent masterpieces, the critic who should take upon himself to pass sentence or pronounce judgment would in my opinion display more audacity than discretion. The steadfast and imperturbable skill of hand which has woven so many threads of incident, so many shades of character, so many changes of intrigue, into so perfect and superb a pattern of incomparable art as dazzles and delights the reader of *The Alchemist* is unquestionably unique—above comparison with any later or earlier example of kindred genius in the whole range of comedy, if not in the whole world of fiction. The manifold harmony of inventive combination and imaginative contrast—the multitudinous unity of various and concordant effects—the complexity and the simplicity of action and impression, which hardly allow the reader's mind to hesitate between enjoyment and astonishment, laughter and wonder, admiration and diversion—all the distinctive qualities which the alchemic cunning of the poet has fused together in the crucible of dramatic satire for the production of a flawless work of art, have given us the most perfect model of imaginative realism and satirical comedy that the world has ever seen; the most wonderful work of its kind that can ever be run upon the same lines. ⟨. . .⟩

—Algernon Charles Swinburne, *A Study of Ben Jonson* (London: Chatto & Windus, 1889): pp. 35–37.

Samuel Coleridge on Jonson's Originality

[Samuel Taylor Coleridge (1772–1834) was an English lyrical poet, philosopher and gifted literary critic. He is the author of the *Lyrical Ballads,* written with William Wordsworth. *His Biographia Literaria* (1817) is esteemed as the most significant work of literary criticism written during the Romantic period. In this excerpt, Coleridge offers general commentary on key characteristics of Jonson's writing, discussing his characters, diction, and relation to his era.]

Ben Jonson is original; he is, indeed, the only one of the great dramatists of that day who was not either directly produced, or very greatly modified, by Shakespeare. In truth, he differs from our great master in everything—in form and in substance—and betrays not tokens of his proximity. He is not original in the same way as Shakespeare is original; but after a fashion of his own, Ben Jonson is most truly original.

The characters in his plays are, in the strictest sense of the term, abstractions. Some very prominent feature is taken from the whole man, and that single feature of humour is made the basis upon which the entire character is built up. Ben Jonson's *dramatis personæ* are almost as fixed as the masks of the ancient actors; you know from the first scene—sometimes from the list of names—exactly what every one of them is to be. He was a very accurately observing man; but he cared only to observe what was external or open to, and likely to impress, the senses. He individualizes, not so much, if at all, by the exhibition of moral or intellectual differences, as by the varieties and contrasts of manners, modes of speech and tricks of temper; as in such characters as Puntarvolo, Bobadill, &c.

I believe there is not one whim or affectation in common life noted in any memoir of that age which may not be found drawn and framed in some corner or other of Ben Jonson's dramas; and they have this merit, in common with Hogarth's prints, that not a single circumstance is introduced in them which does not play upon, and help to bring out, the dominant humour or humours of the piece. Indeed I ought very particularly to call your attention to the extraordinary skill shown by Ben Jonson in contriving situations for the display of his characters. In fact, his care and anxiety in this matter led him to do what scarcely any of the dramatists of that age did— that is, invent his plots. It is not a first perusal that suffices for the full perception of the elaborate artifice of the plots of the *Alchemist* and the *Silent Woman;*—that of the former is absolute perfection for a necessary entanglement, and an unexpected, yet natural, evolution.

Ben Jonson exhibits a sterling English diction, and he has with great skill contrived varieties of construction; but his style is rarely sweet or harmonious, in consequence of his labour at point and strength being so evident. In all his works, in verse and prose, there is an extraordinary opulence of thought; but it is the produce of an amassing power in the author, and not the growth from within.

Indeed a large proportion of Ben Jonson's thoughts may be traced to classic or obscure modern writers, by those who are learned and curious enough to follow the steps of this robust, surly, and observing dramatist.

—Samuel Coleridge, *Coleridge's Literary Criticism* (London: Henry Frowde, 1908): pp. 247–248.

C. H. HERFORD AND PERCY SIMPSON COMPARE SUBTLE AND FACE WITH VOLPONE AND MOSCA

[Herford (1853–1931) and Simpson are co-editors of the exhaustive Oxford *Ben Jonson*. C. H. Herford, Litt.D., Trinity College, is Professor of English Literature in the University of Manchester. He is the author of *Shakespeare and the Arts; Shakespeare; Wordsworth; Robert Browning; The Permanent Power of English Poetry;* and *A Sketch of Recent Shakespearean Investigation, 1892–1923.* Percy Simpson is author of *Studies in Elizabethan Drama, The Theme of Revenge in Elizabethan Tragedies, Proof-Reading in the 16th, 17th and 18th Centuries,* and *Biographical Study of Shakespeare.* In this selection, Herford and Simpson compare Jonson's representations of Subtle and Face with those of Volpone and Mosca.]

⟨. . .⟩ The same insistent realism, with one significant exception, marks the treatment throughout. The *Volpone* type obviously reappears in its structure, but adapted to the demands of a livelier actuality, and of a more genial conception of comic orthodoxy. Volpone yields nothing in knavery to Subtle, but Subtle is despoiled of the explicit poetry which breaks in lurid flashes from the Fox; he comes before us, not chanting an exultant morning hymn to his shrined treasure, 'the world's soul and mine', but exchanging volleys of uncompromising Billingsgate with his partner in iniquity. And this sordid impostor of the north is at bottom far more intelligible than the Venetian patrician. Volpone, so securely incorporated, by his rank and status, with the very body of the Venetian polity, is yet felt to be the alien he is; and Jonson, beyond dubbing with a Venetian title and quality the literary plant he had stuck in the Venetian earth, was at no very great pains to produce the illusion of natural growth. Subtle is bound by no such ties of ostensible community to the society he preys upon, and his operations are far more deeply ingrained with sham; but we are made, none the less, to see that this creature had a natural history, that he is a growth of the soil,—a fungus-growth rooted in the greed and hunger of London. In words of Carlylean flavour and pungency Jonson tells us what his naked root was like:

> At *pie-corner,*
> Taking your meale of steeme in, from cookes stalls,
> Where, like the father of hunger, you did walke
> Piteously costiue, with your pinch'd-horne-nose,
> And your complexion, of the *romane* wash,
> Stuck full of black, and melancholique wormes.

And Subtle remains to the end sordid in his making and spending of money. His present fortune depends on a lucky chance, and he plays his part with the seriousness of one who was hungry yesterday and knows that he may be hungry to-morrow. He has the cunning of the opulent magnifico without his vein of fiendish romance. Volpone's freaks of insolent bravado here become the routine of a cheating trade. He plays the mountebank in a fit of exuberant caprice, Subtle in the sober way of business. The alchemist has indeed his philosophy too, and can expound it in lofty phrases and support it by arguments which silence the sceptic Surly and give pause even to our easy modern scorn for alchemy. Jonson has not been content, like Bruno, to put merely the hocus-pocus verbiage which imposed upon the mob into the mouth of the impostor he sought to confront. Less out of generosity than out of the thorough-going candour of the scholar, he allows him the benefit of the best answer which the wisdom of alchemistic speculation could provide. A practitioner whose methods with the public were subjected to so annihilating an exposure might be allowed to score an intellectual victory over a layman with little risk. But Subtle's philosophy, his phrases, and his arguments are not, in any intimate sense, his own; they are not, like Volpone's, tinged with the humours of an individual mind and temper. They are merely the common property of his bogus order, stock weapons which he handles according to the rules of a conventional sword-craft,—the trade practices of the alchemist quack. Even his sensuality is of a lower deep. Volpone makes base love to a noble woman, Mammon to a base woman whom he thinks noble: Subtle makes base love to Dol Common or Dame Pliant as occasion serves or the 'longest cut at night' decides, and if another man has been before him, it is 'only one man more'.

Face is much more nearly related to Mosca than Subtle to Volpone. But he is far from being a replica. The fabric of make-believe which he sustains is several degrees more complicated and various. Mosca is a real parasite dependent upon a real patron; Face plays alchemist's drudge, as he plays the 'Captain', the joint business in which, at least, he is the more masterful partner and has the larger stake. The energetic opening scene, where the two rogues vie in tearing away the last ragged vesture of each other's self-respect, makes us vividly aware of the natural history of Face no less than of Subtle; Mosca is the parasite of the books and of Roman satire; but Jeremy, the enterprising butler, accomplished in all the varieties of backstair pilfering, who compounds with a conjurer for the use of his master's empty house on the terms of equal profits and a bonus in the shape of 'quarreling dimensions' and 'rules to cheat at horse-race, cock-pit, cards', must have been instantly accepted as a London rascal true to type.

If Face is a Mosca of more shifts and better luck, the third member of the 'indenture tripartite' has no equivalent in the earlier play. The female rogue, paramour and partner of the chief contriver of the harms, was, however, a figure not unknown to Jonson; and in the same qualified sense in which Sejanus may be called a prototype of Face, Livia, his confederate in the death of Drusus, may be called a prototype of Dol. But Livia plays only a passing part, while Dol is an indispensable member of the 'house',—indispensable to the precious pair whose game she plays and whose dangerous feuds she quells, indispensable to the intrigue which she complicates and enriches, indispensable above all to the satire, to the flavour of which her presence adds an ironical pungency not to be otherwise obtained. Even the business of catering for the lust of clients illustrates less drastically the pretension of the alchemist to 'holy living' than do the sordid lotteries and altercations of Subtle and Face for the possession of their common mistress. As a character Dol falls short of being a masterpiece, but she stands in the front rank of Jonson's women, and may be counted one of the best 'Dol Commons' in our literature. Falstaff's mistress, whom Jonson perhaps had in mind, is of course a mere sketch.

—C. H. Herford and Percy Simpson, *Ben Jonson: Volumes I & II, The Man and His Work, The Second Volume* (London: Oxford University Press, 1925): pp. 100–102.

ALVIN B. KERNAN ON THE ALLEGORY OF ALCHEMY IN THE PLAY

[Alvin B. Kernan has served as Professor of English at Yale and Princeton and is a senior advisor in the humanities at the Andrew W. Mellon Foundation. He is the author of numerous books of literary criticism, including Shakespeare, *The King's Playwright in the Stuart Court, 1603–1613; Death of Literature; Modern Satire;* and *Two Renaissance Mythmakers: Christopher Marlowe and Ben Jonson.* He has also authored an academic memoir, *In Plato's Cave* and *Crossing the Line,* a highly praised memoir of his naval service in World War II. In this excerpt, Kernan discusses alchemical transformation as an allegory relating both to the gulls of the play and to Jonson as playwright.]

Despite the variety of abstruse arts practiced by Face and Subtle, alchemy is their defining activity, and from its central position in the play this art of arts interprets all other parts. To begin with the most obvious instance of its interpretive function, the constant presence of the concept of alchemy tells us that what the chemist tries to do with base metal like lead is exactly what each of the characters is trying to do with himself. All of the characters are very ordinary clay, about as low on the scale of humanity as lead is on the scale of metals; but all desire to be transformed into something as rich and rare as gold; Dapper into a great gambler, Kastril into a duelist, Sir Epicure into the Emperor of the world. Jonson was thoroughly aware that alchemy serves as a metaphor for character transformation, and in a number of scenes it is impossible to tell whether the raw materials and processes being discussed refer to people or metals. In the opening scene, for example, where Face and Subtle quarrel, each uses alchemical language to describe the way in which he has raised and "sublimed" the other from dung and poverty to fame and riches. The same sort of thing happens again in II.3.95ff. where it is not at all clear whether Face and Subtle are discussing the stages by which the chemicals are refined and made to yield gold, or whether they are talking about the methods by which the con man in all ages whets his victim's greed in order to take him for the largest possible amount.

In a curious way, what the fools of the play fail to do, the rogues almost achieve. That is, Face and Subtle and Dol do manage to convert the crudest raw materials imaginable, human greed, lust, vanity, and stupidity, into gold by working the fools for all they are worth. If alchemy is ever possible, the play seems to be saying, then its true powers are the wit and the quickness of such clever characters as Face and Subtle, who always manage to turn a dollar somehow. In the end, of course, even these rogues manage to overreach themselves and to lose all the gold and treasure they have stored in the cellar to the master of the house, Lovewit, who returns to town suddenly. But when Lovewit materializes at the beginning of Act V, far from being a *deus ex machina* he is simply the embodiment, in a more respectable form, of that mental agility and histrionic skill, that wit, which we have been watching throughout the play with such fascination as it appears in Face and Subtle, turning the rough opportunities of life into pure gold. Lovewit's marriage with the rich widow and his seizure of all the loot stored in his cellar is the perfect ending of the play, the triumph of true alchemy, the wit which achieves riches and happiness by making the most of such chances as the world throws its way.

—Alvin B. Kernan, Introduction to *Ben Jonson:* The Alchemist (New Haven: Yale University Press, 1974): pp. 12–13.

JOHN DRYDEN ON JONSON AS CLASSICIST

[John Dryden was an English poet, dramatist, and literary critic who wrote almost 30 works for the stage, number of translations, and the critical study *An Essay on Dramatic Poesy.* In this excerpt, Dryden discusses Jonson's debt to classical writers, examining his comic works and comparing him to Shakespeare.]

As for Jonson, to whose character I am now arrived, if we look upon him while he was himself (for his last plays were but his dotages), I think him the most learned and judicious writer which any theatre ever had. He was a most severe judge of himself as well as others. One cannot say he wanted wit, but rather that he was frugal of it. In his works you find little to retrench or alter. Wit, and language, and humour also in some measure, we had before him; but something of art was wanting to the drama till he came. He managed his strength to more advantage than any who preceded him. You seldom find him making love in any of his scenes, or endeavouring to move the passions; his genius was too sullen and saturnine to do it gracefully, especially when he knew he came after those who had performed both to such an height. Humour was his proper sphere; and in that he delighted most to represent mechanic people. He was deeply conversant in the Ancients, both Greek and Latin, and he borrowed boldly from them: there is scarce a poet or historian among the Roman authors of those times whom he has not translated in *Sejanus* and *Catiline*. But he has done his robberies so openly that one may see he fears not to be taxed by any law. He invades authors like a monarch, and what would be theft in other poets is only victory in him. With the spoils of these writers he so represents old Rome to us, in its rites, ceremonies, and customs, that if one of their poets had written either of his tragedies, we had seen less of it than in him. If there was any fault in his language, 'twas that he weaved it too closely and laboriously in his serious plays: perhaps, too, he did a little too much romanize our tongue, leaving the words which he translated almost as much Latin as he found them: wherein, though he learnedly followed the idiom of their language, he did not enough comply with ours. If I would compare him with Shakespeare, I must acknowledge him the more correct poet, but Shakespeare the greater wit. Shakespeare was the Homer, or father of our dramatic poets; Jonson was the Virgil, the pattern of elaborate writing; I admire him, but I love Shakespeare. To conclude of him, as he has given us the most correct plays, so in the precepts which he has laid down in his *Discoveries,* we have as many and profitable rules for perfecting the stage as any wherewith the French can furnish us.

—John Dryden, *Of Dramatic Poesy and Other Critical Essays* (London: Dent, 1962): pp. 69–70.

IAN DONALDSON ON THE SIGNIFICANCE OF TIMING IN THE PLAY

[Professor Ian Donaldson is Chair of the Faculty of English, and Fellow of King's College, Cambridge. From 1969 to 1991 he was Professor of English at the Australian National University, Canberra, and from 1991 to 1994 Regius Professor of Rhetoric and English Literature at the University of Edinburgh. He is a General Editor of *The Cambridge Edition of the Works of Ben Jonson,* and a Consultant Editor for the *New Dictionary of National Biography.* His published scholarship covers Jonson and Shakespeare, Renaissance comedy, and modern European drama. In this except Donaldson discusses how the theme of timing contributes to Jonson's comic effect.]

⟨. . .⟩ An examination of the organization of time in *The Alchemist* does more, however, than reveal Jonson's great cleverness in dramatic engineering, for it will also be evident that time, and the attitudes which people display towards it, are a central preoccupation of the play. The comedy's formal structure elegantly bears and enacts a central theme: as in *Volpone,* Jonson explores the nature of human expectation, and the various ways in which people hope, 'Each greedy minute' (I.i.80), to have their most covetous dreams fulfilled. In Shakespearian comedy time often operates as a benign and clarifying force, dispelling error, rewarding devotion, and restoring that which is lost. It is to this property in time that the characters, at their most bewildered, often make appeal:

> O Time, thou must untangle this, not I;
> It is too hard a knot for me t'untie.
>
> (*Twelfth Night*, II. ii. 38–9)

> Well, Time is the old justice that examines all such
> offenders, and let Time try.
>
> (*As You Like It*, IV. i. 178–80)

In *The Alchemist* time is viewed in other ways. For many of the characters, time is a commodity in which it is profitable to invest. Expectation may be governed by self-interest, while couched in the language of devotion: 'But how long time, / Sir, must the *Saints* expect, yet?' (III.ii.125–6). The comedy reveals bizarre correspondences between the views of time taken by characters of apparently contrary temperament and disposition: between the Puritans' apocalyptic habits of mind, and the sensuous expectations of Sir Epicure Mammon; between the gambling instincts of Dapper, and those of Face and Subtle; between Kastril's manner of living for the moment, and that of the rogues with whom he finds himself allied. To examine the time-scheme of *The Alchemist* is to discover more fully what the play is centrally about. ⟨. . .⟩

Jonson's preference for working theatrically within the 'fit bounds' of time and place did not derive from pedantry, or blind adherence to classical practice, or failure to understand the more variable ways in which the dramatic imagination might be called into play. Such 'bounds' worked rather as a powerful stimulus to his comic invention, and his wry and complex vision of the world; a world that ran—almost, yet significantly for the comic dramatist, not quite—like a perfect clock.

—Ian Donaldson, *Jonson's Magic Houses: Essays in Interpretation*, (Oxford: Clarendon Press, 1997): pp. 102–103, 105.

Plot Summary of
Bartholomew Fair

Bartholomew Fair, the fourth of Jonson's great comedies is an exuberant holiday play presenting a profusion of colorful characters, overlapping plot lines, and riotous entertainments. Unifying the multiplicity of persons and events is the fair itself, which, like the play, offers amusements to its attendants, inspiring their curiosity, delight and disdain. Many critics have thus interpreted the play as a defense of Jonson's art, understanding the fair as a metaphor for the theater. From the opening **Induction** scene, the play challenges audience members to consider their own role as spectators and aesthetic and moral judges.

The Induction's intimate address to the audience immediately establishes an explicit relationship between the figures on the stage and those in the audience. The Scribner formally reads "Articles of Agreement" between audience members and the playwright.

Act I opens as the jolly proctor John Littlewit chuckles over the marriage license he prepared for Bartholomew Cokes, who will be married on "Bartholomew Day." Littlewit and his wife Win-the-Fight are joined by Winwife, who is wooing Win-the-Fight's mother, Dame Purecraft. Advising Winwife to act mad, they explain that Purecraft was persuaded by fortunetellers to believe that her happiness depends upon marrying a madman within the week. They discuss the madcap Quarlous and the baker turned prophet, Puritan Zeal-of-the-Land Busy, who courts Purecraft.

Quarlous arrives and the group discusses the fanatic Busy, until Humphrey Wasp, "the terrible, testy, old servant"(I.iv.40) to Cokes enters, officiously requesting Cokes' marriage license. To great comic effect, Wasp describes his travails working for his foolish, immature master, whom he governs as much as serves.

Cokes arrives with his fiancée, Grace and Mistress Overdo, wife of the justice of the peace. To Wasp's frustration, Cokes resolutely declares that the group will attend Bartholomew Fair. Winwife and Quarlous jest about the idiotic Cokes and his irritable servant and decide to follow them to the fair for further sport.

Meanwhile, Littlewit, desiring to have his puppet play performed at the fair, devises a scheme to persuade Purecraft and Busy to allow the family to attend the "profane" event. He instructs Win to feign an acute longing to eat the roast pig sold at the fair. In an amusing depiction of religious hypocrisy, Jonson portrays Purecraft's and Busy's initial, overzealous repudiation of the fair, prohibited by Puritan strictures, and their subsequent rationalization of attending the event and eating pig.

In **Act II**, Justice Overdo smugly relishes his plan to attend the fair disguised as a madman and apprehend the illicit activities transpiring there. Jonson introduces several colorful characters of the fair, including, Trash, the gingerbread lady, Leatherhead, a toy man, Nightingale, a ballad singer, and Ursula, the pig roaster, who emerges from her booth raucously complaining about the toil of her work. Suspecting misconduct at Ursula's booth, Overdo stops there, drinking and talking with an array of dubious characters who assume he is the mad Arthur of Bradley. Failing to understand the slang of Ursula's assistant Mooncalf, Overdo mistakes the cunning thief Edgworth for a civil young man, corrupted by bad influences. He resolves to "rescue [him] out of the hands of the lewd man and the strange woman" (II.v.61–2).

Quarlous and Winwife arrive at the Fair, observing with amusement and arrogance the vendors around them. Stopping at Ursula's booth, their rude gibes provoke her to a hilarious array of vituperative insults until she brings out her scalding pan, threatening to throw hot oil at them. She falls, burning her leg, and Knockem, friend to Ursula, offers to man her booth so that she can sit while watching over the business.

As Cokes, Wasp, Grace, Mistress Overdo, and the disguised Overdo explore the fair, Edgworth steals Cokes' purse from his pocket. Discovering he has been robbed, Cokes is hardly distraught, as it was "not [his] best purse" (II.vi.107). With Edgworth nearby, he proudly declares that he defies the thief to try again, placing his "good purse" in his pocket. Wasp, suspecting Overdo to be the thief, beats him.

In **Act III**, Quarlous and Littlewit watch with amusement as Busy guides Purecraft, Littlewit and Win through the fair, urging the group not to look at the booths', "baits" "hung out on every side to catch [them]" (III.ii.38). Reaching Ursula's booth, they eat pig.

To the dismay of the exasperated Wasp, Cokes impulsively decides to buy Leatherhead's and Trash's entire stock of toys and ginger-bread, planning to use the goods during the wedding masque and banquet. As Cokes is captivated by Nightingale's ballad, which admonishes listeners to beware of thieves, Edgworth again picks his pocket, and Quarlous and Littlewit watch with delight. Overdo is again suspected for the crime and the officials seize him. Leveraging his knowledge of Edgworth's crime, Quarlous instructs him to steal Cokes' marriage license from Wasp.

Now that his "belly is full" (III.vi.44) with pig, Busy vehemently condemns the fair. In his escalating fury, Busy attempts to destroy the merchandise of Trash and Letterhead, which he calls an "idola-trous grove of images" and is seized by the officers.

In **Act IV**, Jonson introduces Trouble-All, a lawyer driven mad because Justice Overdo dislodged him from his position in the courts. Unwilling to act without Overdo's approval, he tries to pre-vent the officers from putting "Bradley" in the stocks without the Justice's warrant. Determined to get whatever they can out of the naïve Cokes, Edgworth and Nightingale trick him out of his sword and cloak. As Cokes laments that he is bereft of his money and lost from his companions, he begins to realize that he has been cheated repeatedly at the fair.

Grace has declared she cannot endure marriage with Cokes and Quarlous and Winwife are ready to fight each other for her hand. Grace asserts that she would rather leave the choice up to destiny in a gentler contest: each man is to write a word on a pad, which she will show to a passerby, asking him to mark his favorite word. The man who wrote the marked word will win her. Trouble-All walks by and chooses a word, which Grace resolves to keep secret until they return home.

Edgworth steals the marriage license from Wasp while he is engaged in an argument. As the group's game of vapours escalates into a fight, Knockem steals their cloaks and swords and flees the scene. After he audaciously challenges their authority, guards seize Wasp.

Littlewit leaves Win with Captain Jordan and Captain Whit, who, with Knockem and Ursula, conceive a plan to persuade the women into dressing up as prostitutes. Mistaking Mistress Overdo for a high-class prostitute, and therefore commercial competition, the whore Ramping Alice attacks her.

The prisoners Wasp, Overdo, and Busy are put in the stocks. Wasp quickly escapes. While the officer is being attacked by Trouble-All for proceeding without Overdo's warrant, Busy and Overdo also escape. In the midst of the chaos, Purecraft declares her ardent love for the madman, Trouble-All.

In **Act V**, Quarlous disguises himself to look like Trouble-All and Purecraft, fooled, tries to woo him. Grace reveals that Winwife's word was chosen and he has thus won her. As Quarlous reasons that he should marry Purecraft for her money, Overdo, eager to help the man he has driven mad, gives Quarlous, whom he mistakes for Trouble-All, a blank warrant.

Cokes arrives at the puppet show and meets the "actors," taking great delight in the puppets. As Littlewit departs to find his wife, Winwife and Grace appear at the performance, and moments later Knockem, Whit, Edgworth, and the masked Mistress Overdo, Win and Wasp arrive. Leatherhead presents *Hero and Leander*, vulgarized and adapted by Littlewit to be "easy and modern for the times." Busy begins to fervently denounce the "profane" puppets, and Leatherhead proposes that Busy debate this matter with the puppet Dionysus. Busy is defeated by the puppet, to great comic effect. Declaring that he has witnessed enough enormity, Overdo reveals his identity, mildly reproaching Wasp, Cokes, Busy, Leatherhead, Knockem, and Whit. Almost all of the play's many plot lines are hastily resolved: Overdo unmasks Win; Trouble-All enters naked and Quarlous confesses to stealing his clothes and impersonating him; Overdo discovers that one of the masked ladies is his wife; Quarlous reveals to Overdo who the real cutpurse is, and displays for Wasp the stolen license. Overdo, acting on his resolution to be a more compassionate justice, and having learned humility by experiencing his own folly throughout the day, amicably invites the entire group to come to his house for supper. ❁

List of Characters in
Bartholomew Fair

Bartholomew Cokes is a fatuous and infantile young squire whose naiveté and trusting affability makes him the victim of cheaters and thieves at the fair. However, Cokes' well meaning interest and enthusiasm toward the people and novelties around him add a compelling element to his character; Ursula and the other characters of the fair are so vibrant that some part of the reader wants to abandon the critical eye and social prejudices of the other characters and dive into the fun with Cokes.

Mistress Grace Wellborn, ward of the Justice Adam Overdo, was purchased by Overdo and, against her desires, forced to marry Cokes. She is a sober, sharp-sighted woman whose discreet intelligence gets her out of her loathed engagement and wins her a new spouse.

Dame Purecraft, widowed mother of Win-the-Fight, is "a most elect hypocrite" (I.v.144) who pretends to be a pious Puritan for her own gain. Convinced by fortune tellers that she must marry the madman, she is courted by Busy and Winwife, but, at the fair, suddenly falls in love with the madman Trouble-All. At the close of the play, she agrees to marry Quarlous.

Humphrey Wasp, servant to Cokes, is true to his name: he flies about in his officious haste, buzzes in his chatter and stings with his proud retorts and angry reproaches of Cokes. Exasperated and embarrassed by Coke's frivolity and gullibility, he rebukes his charge throughout the play. Defining himself as a supremely responsible governor, Wasp is mortified to have been put in the stocks and confounded when he learns that the marriage license was stolen from him.

Zeal-of-the-Land Busy, a baker turned Puritan prophet, is a suitor to Dame Purecraft, and an overzealous hypocrite whose vehement censure of the fair provides amusement for audiences as well as for the other characters of the play. Perhaps he is best described by Quarlous who calls him "a notable hypocritical vermin" (I.iii.123), explaining that he "stands upon his face more than his faith, at all times; ever in seditious motion, and reproving for vain-glory; of a most lunatic conscience and spleen, and affects the violence of singularity in all he does" (I.iii.124–6).

John Littlewit, a proctor and husband to Win-the-Fight, is the author of a puppet play that he hopes to have performed at the fair. A jocose, empty-headed figure, Littlewit conceives insipid jokes and schemes throughout the play. His puppet play is a combination of the stories of Hero and Leander and Damon and Pythias, both of which are sullied by Littlewit's low humor.

Adam Overdo, a meddling, self-important justice of the peace, goes about the fair disguised as a fool, seeking out enormity. Overly proud of his own device, Overdo conceives his pursuit of justice as an extremely valiant and grave endeavor. His experiences at the fair lead him to become a more compassionate justice, who humbly embraces his own folly and capacity for misjudgment.

Ursula is the owner of the pig roasting booth at the fair. Perhaps the most vibrant and exciting of Jonson's creations in this play, the greasy, obese Ursula raucously complains, insults, and curses with wonderful vituperative wit. Frank and bold, Ursula's raving complaints and abuses delight.

Win-the-Fight Littlewit, is the timid wife of Littlewit, who contentedly follows her husband's proposal, pretending to suffer from a severe longing for pig. She is tricked by Captain Whit into wearing a green dress, which signifies that she is a prostitute. Whit offers her to other men, but she is reunited with her husband at the puppet show before coming to any harm.

Quarlous is a gamester and madcap who, with Winwife, observes in amusement the folly of Cokes and the others at the fair. Witty, pragmatic, and arrogant, Quarlous simulates more madness than he truly suffers. He conspires with Edgworth, employing him to steal Wasp's marriage license, and disguises himself as Trouble-All in an attempt to win Dame Purecraft.

Winwife, perhaps more sensible than his friend Quarlous, but certainly less witty, is introduced in Act I as a suitor to Dame Purecraft. At the fair, however, he competes with Quarlous for Grace, and true to his name, wins her as his wife.

Trouble-All, the madman, was an officer in the Court of Piepowders and was dislodged from his position by Overdo. Driven to distraction after this incident, he will do nothing without Overdo's warrant. ❀

Critical Views on
Bartholomew Fair

BEN JONSON ON THE DIDACTIC PURPOSES OF COMEDY

[Benjamin Jonson was an English Jacobean dramatist, poet, and literary critic. Regarded as the second most important English dramatist, after William Shakespeare, Jonson was esteemed as a erudite man of letters and gifted playwright. His major plays include the comedies *Every Man in His Humour* (1598), *Volpone* (1606), *The Alchemist* (1610), and *Bartholomew Fair* (1614). In this excerpt, Jonson discusses comedy's didactic function and explores the problems with the low humor that amused the popular audiences of his day.]

The parts of a comedy are the same with a tragedy, and the end is partly the same. For they both delight and teach; the comics are called *didaskaloi* of the Greeks, no less than the tragics.

Nor is the moving of laughter always the end of comedy, that is rather a fowling for the people's delight, or their fooling. For, as Aristotle says rightly, the moving of laughter is a fault in comedy, a kind of turpitude that depraves some part of man's nature without a disease. As a wry face without pain moves laughter, or a deformed vizard, or a rude clown dressed in a lady's habit and using her actions: we dislike and scorn such representations, which made the ancient philosophers ever think laughter unfitting in a wise man. And this induced Plato to esteem of Homer as a sacrilegious person, because he presented the gods sometimes laughing. As also it is divinely said of Aristotle, that to seem ridiculous is a part of dishonesty and foolish.

So that what, either in the words or sense of an author, or in the language or actions of men, is awry or depraved, doth strangely stir mean affections and provoke for the most part to laughter. And therefore it was clear that all insolent and obscene speeches; jest upon the best men; injuries to particular persons; perverse and sinister sayings (and the rather unexpected) in the old comedy did move laughter, especially where it did imitate any dishonesty. And scurrility came forth in the place of wit, which who understands the nature and genius of laughter cannot but perfectly know.

Of which Aristophanes affords an ample harvest, having not only outgone Plautus or any other in that kind, but expressed all the moods and figures of what is ridiculous, oddly. In short, as vinegar is not accounted good until the wine be corrupted, so jests that are true and natural seldom raise laughter with the beast, the multitude. They love nothing that is right and proper; the farther it runs from reason or possibility, with them, the better it is.

What could have made them laugh like to see Socrates presented, that example of all good life, honesty, and virtue, to have him hoisted up with a pulley and there play the philosopher in a basket, measure how many foot a flea could skip geometrically by a just scale, and edify the people from the engine? This was theatrical wit, right stage-jesting, and relishing a playhouse, invented for scorn and laughter; whereas, if it had savored of equity, truth, perspicuity, and candor, to have tasted a wise or a learned palate, spit it out presently. "This is bitter and profitable, this instructs and would inform us; what need we know anything, that are nobly born, more than a horse race or a hunting match, our day to break with citizens, and such innate mysteries."

This is truly leaping from the stage to the tumbril again, reducing all wit to the original dung-cart.

—*Discoveries* from "The 1640 Folio edition of Jonson's Works" in *Ben Jonson's Plays and Masques*, 2nd ed., ed. Richard Harp (New York: W. W. Norton, 2001): pp. 354–355.

C. H. HERFORD AND PERCY SIMPSON ON THE FAIR AS THE TRUE SUBJECT OF THE PLAY

[Herford (1853–1931) and Simpson are co-editors of the exhaustive Oxford *Ben Jonson*. C. H. Herford, Litt.D., Trinity College, is Professor of English Literature in the University of Manchester. He is the author of *Shakespeare and the Arts; Shakespeare; Wordsworth; Robert Browning; The Permanent Power of English Poetry;* and *A Sketch of Recent Shakespearean Investigation, 1892–1923.* Percy Simpson is author of *Studies in Elizabethan Drama, The Theme of Revenge in Elizabethan Tragedies, Proof-Reading in the 16th, 17th and 18th Centuries,* and *Biographical Study of Shakespeare.* In this selection, Herford and Simpson discuss differences in Jonson's style in *Bartholomew Fair* and comment on the fair as the ultimate and unifying concern of the play.]

The impersonal severity, the censorious sternness, which make comedies like *Volpone* and even *The Alchemist* but equivocal examples of the comic spirit, have as far as the playgoing public are concerned wholly vanished from *Bartholomew Fair.* The preacher has descended from his pulpit, the censor has stripped off the robes of his authority and of his chartered scorn; he mingles with the people, with the mob of 'ordinary readers' and the vaster mob of the unreading and the cannot-read, takes part in their least refined exhibitions and amusements and, as the chief exhibition of all, pillories for their ridicule the embodiments of the censorious spirit itself. The Induction at once betrays and announces this changed disposition. Instead of branding his public, in an 'armed Prologue', as ignorant enemies of art if they found his play dull, or swearing the play was good 'and if you like't you may', he now makes a genial compact with them to the effect that 'euery person here (shall) haue his or their free-will of censure, to like or dislike at their owne charge, the *Author* hauing now departed with his right.' ⟨...⟩

⟨...⟩ But in the artistry of *Bartholomew Fair* the last trace of artifice has vanished. The lines of cleavage between the tricksters and the dupes, which so largely determine the structure of Jonsonian comedy, are here unusually complicated. The comic harms come about inevitably, as natural incidents of the Fair, without the intervention of a professional contriver called Brainworm or Buffone. Of palpable literary reminiscence in the plot-making there is hardly a trace. Whatever nutriment Jonson has drawn from Plautus has passed into the blood and been converted into nerve and tissue. We have not to do with Plautine cunning slaves and boastful soldiers more or less cleverly disguised, but with unadulterated English roguery and vagabondage, as they grew and throve in the ripe soil of the great London show. The Fair is indeed the true subject of the play, the salient, obsessive, uncircumventable, ubiquitous fact to which all the bewildering multiplicity of persons and interests have relation. There is no hero, no dominant character, no well-defined unity of plot; but the Fair, which has brought all this motley multitude together, and set in motion their legion of appetencies, provides a real unity of theme and tone, analogous in its realist fashion to that imposed by the enchanted woodlands of Athens or of Arden upon the throngs of incommensurable creatures—fairies, artisans, antique heroes and courtiers, or shepherds of pastoral and of real life—who meet and mingle in its shades. For every class of London citizen it offers some kind of allurement. To some it is a forbidden paradise of ungodly savours and shows, to some an unweeded garden crying for the hoe, to some an unequalled place of business, where rotten goods can be got rid of, and fools exploited, more easily than elsewhere; regular *habitués,* practising their venerable frauds and well-tried recipes for profit or plunder, jostle with novices who have ventured curiously over the threshold of iniquity, with austere reformers in quest of matter for the hurdle or the pillory, with gentle-folks who look on disdainfully at the gross amusements, but still look on. Like the laboratory of Subtle, the Fair lays all sorts and conditions of men under its spell; and the main source of comedy lies in the disasters which befall the adventurous or curious explorers from outside.

> —C. H. Herford and Percy Simpson, *Ben Jonson: Volumes I & II, The Man and His Work, The Second Volume* (London: Oxford University Press, 1925): pp. 132–133, 137–138.

Harry Levin on Shakespeare, Jonson and Realism in *Bartholomew Fair*

[Harry Levin (1912–93), Irving Babbitt Professor of Comparative Literature at Harvard University, authored numerous books of literary criticism, including *James Joyce: A Critical Introduction* and *Contexts of Criticism* as well as *The Overreacher,* Levin's Study on Christopher Marlowe. In this excerpt, Levin comments generally on differences in Shakespeare's and Jonson's approaches to playwrighting and discusses Jonson's realism in *Bartholomew Fair*.]

The demands of realism are most fully satisfied by *Bartholomew Fair*. Although the most meticulously local of Jonson's plays, it is also the most broadly universal; for is not all the world a fair— paraphrasing Seneca, Jonson develops the conceit in his *Discoveries*—and do not men seek gilded roofs and marble pillars, even as children are attracted to cockleshells and hobby-horses? Under this more genial dispensation, humours diffuse into vapours, and vapours evaporate *in fumo*. Like a pilgrimage, a fair forms a comprehensive natural background against which all types and classes may be exhibited; like Chaucer, Jonson allows his characters to step out of the proscenium. Ursula, the pig-woman, challenges an odorous comparison with the Wife of Bath herself, let alone Elinor Rumming or Marion Tweedy Bloom. Here as always, realism thrives upon the implicit contrast between the way things are presented and the way literature has been in the habit of presenting those same things. What, then, could be a crueller falling-off than for Leander, having swum the Hellespont from Sestos to Abydos, to let a foul-mouthed ferryman row him across the Thames from the Bankside to Puddle Wharf? ⟨. . .⟩

Jonson takes more for granted than Shakespeare does. He presupposes that life is fundamentally a compact, rational affair, needlessly complicated by impulse and artifice. To Shakespeare, all experience, however variegated, is of the same baseless fabric. The two poets, who worked so closely together, were as far apart as Heraclitus and Parmenides. Jonson adopts the attitude of society, Shakespeare the viewpoint of the individual, which is finally more real. Jonson's instrument is logic, Shakespeare's psychology; Jonson's method has been called mechanical, Shakespeare's organic. That is why we must criticize Shakespeare in terms of movement and warmth, Jonson in terms of pattern and colour. ⟨. . .⟩

In his fecundity and in his artificiality, in his virtues and in his faults, Jonson remains the craftsman. When he appraises the idle apprentice Shakespeare, he speaks with the authority of a fellow craftsman, and—after a few precise couplets of prefatory remarks, acknowledgments, and qualifications—deliberately turns on the lyric strain:

> 'I therefore will begin. Soul of the age!
> The applause, delight, the wonder of our stage!'

And he proceeds to a workmanlike and reasonably impassioned estimate. Because he was in the habit of discussing his craft concretely, he could not fail to be interested in Plutarch's comparison of poetry and painting. It is no mere chance that any effort to describe his own work falls repeatedly into the vocabulary of the fine arts. If we are looking for a single impression of Ben Jonson, it is of the Flemish painters that we are finally mindful—of crowded street scenes and rich interiors, of sharp portraiture and lavish ornament, of the gloss and the clarity and the tactile values that are the tokens of mastery.

> —Harry Levin, Introduction to *Ben Jonson: Selected Works* (New York: Random House, 1938): pp. 21, 25, 36.

EUGENE WAITH ON THE "DELICATE BALANCE" IN THE PLAY

[Eugene M. Waith is the Douglas Tracy Smith Professor Emeritus of English Literature at Yale University. He is the author of *Ideas of Greatness; Heroic Drama in England, Shakespeare: The Histories; A Collection of Critical Essays;* and *Patterns and Perspectives in English Renaissance Drama.* Eugene Waith discusses Jonsonian innovations in style, characterization and plot in the play, exploring Jonson's delicate balance of a multitude of diverse voices demonstrated as one of his greatest achievements in the play.]

Ben Jonson is at his best in Bartholomew Fair. His prose has its distinctive combination of grotesque exuberance and iron control. His perceptions are at their sharpest, as he records all the odd details which fasten the play to seventeenth-century London—customs, habits of speech, bits of local gossip, reference to recent events—and the eye which sees this surface so clearly also sees through it to what is archetypal. Without losing any of its particularity, the Fair presents us with the very patterns of folly. Jonson's characterization is as varied and lively as in any of his plays and his comic invention runs on to the end as if it could never tire. ⟨. . .⟩

⟨N⟩o single character dominates ⟨the play⟩ to provide the intense focus of interest found in the other three. Even Ursula, massive and brilliant creation that she is, does not control the action like Volpone or Subtle, whose machinations constantly fascinate at the same time that they repel. Nor is she, like Morose in *Epicoene,* the chief "blocking character" (to use Northrop Frye's term) against whom the whole strategy of the plot is planned and most of the satiric barbs directed. Ursula's booth is indeed a central point from which most of the chicanery and corruption of the Fair radiate, but the active agents are her accomplices, Knockem and Whit, Edgworth and Nightingale, who are less dependent on her than are Dol and Face on Subtle in *The Alchemist.* Among these various imposers upon society in *Bartholomew Fair* interest is more diffused than it is in the preceding comedies.

Furthermore, the direction of the satirical thrust is less immediately clear. ⟨. . .⟩ In *Bartholomew Fair,* satirical exposure of the tricksters who impose on Bartholomew Cokes and, to a lesser extent, on Mistress Overdo and Mistress Littlewit, is balanced by ridicule of Justice Overdo and Rabbi Busy, the arch-enemies of the tricksters. In the conclusion the enemies of the Fair are exposed even more mercilessly than the swindlers within it, and the laughter is at the expense of knaves, gulls, and reformers alike. Not only is none of the main characters truly sympathetic, but the attitudes satirized seem, in a sense, to cancel each other out. One is obliged to make a more complex judgment on the folly of the play than scorn for a preposterous tyrant or the orthodox condemnation of greed. Both in the mechanics of its plot and in the satirical view which they support, *Bartholomew Fair* is a more complex comedy than those which preceded it.

Finally, it may be that the style of this play has seemed deficient when compared to the accepted examples of Jonson's best. Style, for anyone so conscious of literary decorum as Jonson, is so intimately related to setting that one can hardly be surprised if the prose of his Smithfield lacks the grace of the poetry he devised for the Venetian splendors of *Volpone.* ⟨. . .⟩ In the prose of *Bartholomew Fair* it is appropriateness which is emphasized. Though there are a few splendid set pieces, such as Quarlous' diatribe against widows and Overdo's oration against tobacco, Jonson goes further in the direction of realistic dialogue than in most of his other plays. The subtle modulations of this style constitute a major achievement, but one which is more apparent after a second or third reading than at the first.

The brief comparisons I have made suggest that the success of *Bartholomew Fair* is more dependent on the expert joining of many pieces than upon the shaping of any one of them; that its comic structure is complex—a delicate balance of forces; and that its style, marked by verisimilitude, is also less distinguished by single brilliant strokes than by the adjustments which make a unified verbal texture out of the clearly distinct voices of many characters. To this general impression of superbly ordered multiplicity one must add another, of outstanding vitality, for no comedy of Jonson's—perhaps none of any author's—exudes more of the "life force" which Bernard Shaw so admired. Old Ursula sweating profusely in her pig-booth, "all fire and fat," is the perfect emblem of this force, but there is hardly a character who does not share in it. It is the nature of a fair to be all movement—to be popping with activities of every sort—and the vitality of the play, as well as its complexity, is therefore directly related to Jonson's choice of this milieu.

—Eugene W. Waith, Introduction to *Ben Jonson:* Bartholomew Fair, (New Haven: Yale University Press, 1963): pp. 1–4.

EDWARD B. PARTRIDGE ON JONSON'S CRITIQUE OF
LAWGIVERS IN THE PLAY

[Edward B. Partridge is Professor of English Emeritus at Tulane University. He has written the classic *The Broken Compass: A Study of the Major Comedies of Ben Jonson,* and edited an edition of *Bartholomew Fair.* In this excerpt, Partridge offers historical and cultural background information on the fair and discusses how the plot of the play is organized so as to highlight the folly of the traditional lawgivers of English society.]

⟨. . .⟩ But the comic design is more complicated than a simple gulling of the gulls, as a synoptic view of the plot may indicate. In the first act the citizens, the country gentry, and the gentlemen of the town are assembled at the house of Littlewit. Only Justice Overdo is not presented until the second act, which he opens by announcing that he is going to discover and put down the enormities of the Fair. The rest of this act is given over to the folk of the Fair and to two sets of visitors. First, Quarlous and Winwife, the most sophisticated of the visitors, contemptuously view the booth of Ursula and quarrel with her. Second, Cokes and his entourage enter; after Cokes's small purse is stolen, Wasp, suspecting him, beats the innocent Overdo. The third act repeats the second with some remarkable parallels and differences. The third set of visitors, the Littlewits, Dame Purecraft, and Busy, enter. Once again, a purse of Cokes' is stolen—the larger one this time. Once again, Overdo is suspected, but this time taken away under arrest. Just as the second act ends with the beating of Overdo, so the third ends with the arrest of Busy for having thrown over Joan Trash's gingerbread. Violence, gradually growing in the first three acts, explodes in the "vapors" of the fourth act. Here the contentiousness is most shrill. Cokes loses cloak, hat, and sword. Wasp, with irascible joy, enters into the game of vapors. Quarlous quarrels first with Winwife over Grace, then with Cutting over a circle on the ground. Punk Alice beats Mrs. Overdo because she thinks the rich ladies with their velvet haunches are taking her occupation away from her. The act ends with Wasp, Busy, and Overdo being put in the stocks, from which all soon escape. In the final act come the discoveries, most of which deflate. In the puppet show Busy is silenced by Dionysius. Quarlous gains a rich widow at the expense of Busy; Winwife, a lovely wife at the expense of Cokes. Overdo, like an *asinus ex cathedra,* reveals all that he has discovered about the others only to find himself humbled in turn by Quarlous and by his drunken wife. The comedy ends, as comedies about a Fair should, with a feast.

The plot is organized, then, to expose not merely the folly of the obviously foolish Cokes and Littlewits, but also the more harmful folly of the lawgivers—the "dry nurse," Wasp, the Puritan Busy with his loud braying of biblical phrases literally understood, and the magistrate Overdo with his philippics against ale and tobacco. The "careful fool" or the "serious ass," as Quarlous tells us when talking about Wasp, "takes pains to be one, and plays the fool, with the greatest diligence that can be." Grace claims that her guardian, Justice Overdo, is such a fool. Both she and Quarlous distinguish the careful from the careless fool like Cokes—innocent, unstudied, witless Cokes, one of nature's numbskulls. The careful fools are all figures of authority, and each is finally stripped of a large measure of his authority. Wasp is exposed as a master without self-mastery; Busy, a preacher without sense or sincerity; and Overdo, a judge without tolerance or judiciousness.

—Edward B. Partridge, ed., Introduction to *Bartholomew Fair*, by Ben Jonson (Lincoln, Nebraska: University of Nebraska Press, 1964): pp. xi–xii.

IAN DONALDSON ON THE PLAY'S SUBMISSION TO "POPULAR TYRANNY"

[Professor Ian Donaldson is Chair of the Faculty of English, and Fellow of King's College, Cambridge. From 1969 to 1991 he was Professor of English at the Australian National University, Canberra, and from 1991 to 1994 Regius Professor of Rhetoric and English Literature at the University of Edinburgh. He is a General Editor of *The Cambridge Edition of the Works of Ben Jonson,* and a Consultant Editor for the *New Dictionary of National Biography.* His published scholarship covers Jonson and Shakespeare, Renaissance comedy, and modern European drama. In the excerpt, Donaldson argues that through the complexity of its plot and tone, *Bartholomew Fair* simultaneously satisfies and critiques expectations of the popular audience.]

It is sometimes said that in *Bartholomew Fair* Jonson seems to relax the full seriousness and formal control that he had shown in his earlier major comedies, *Volpone* and *The Alchemist,* and that the play belongs to a lower, altogether less serious order of comedy. L. C. Knights, for instance, in an influential essay on Jonson, relegates the play along with *Epicoene* to 'the category of stage entertainments' in which 'the fun is divorced from any rich significance'. Yet there are some oddities about this view of the play as a simple and amiable piece of theatrical fun. Perhaps the first thing one notices about *Bartholomew Fair* is its length and intricacy, the manner in which events crowd in with something of the organized congestion of, say, *The Way of the World*, demanding an intellectual attentiveness different in kind from that usually exacted by the simpler kinds of comedy. The narrative complexity of *Bartholomew Fair* is matched by a complexity of tone. Like *Epicoene*, *Bartholomew Fair* is often described as a genial play, in which Jonson's accustomed harshness gives way to a new moral and theatrical humility. In some obvious ways this description is true; yet it is impossible to miss the irony and hostility behind Jonson's apparently concessive remarks in the Induction that the play is written just to the '*Meridian*' of the Stage-Keeper and of 'the vnderstanding Gentlemen o' the ground'; such gentlemen had damned *Catiline* three years earlier, and were 'understanding' only in the sense that they stood in the pit. Jonson seems now to acknowledge the fact that 'the Drama's Laws the Drama's Patrons give', and to propose a new play written to these laws; yet at the same time he allows us to sense his contempt for such popular tyranny, and his higher valuation of other dramatic laws:

> If there bee neuer a *Seruant-monster* i' the *Fayre*; who can helpe it? he sayes; nor a nest of *Antiques*? Hee is loth to make Nature afraid in his *Playes*, like those that beget *Tales, Tempests*, and such like *Drolleries*, to mixe his head with other mens heeles, let the concupisence of *Iigges* and *Dances*, raigne as strong as it will amongst you: yet if the *Puppets* will please any body, they shall be entreated to come in. (127–34)

The criticism of Shakespeare's use of romance convention, though seriously made, is curiously neutralized as Jonson shifts his ground with deliberate absurdity: the playwright who is loth to make nature afraid now professes himself equally loth to displease his paying audience (perhaps it is no accident that the puppets are later referred to as 'monsters': III.i.12,V.iv.28). Mixing 'his head with other mens heeles' is exactly what Jonson himself will do in *Bartholomew Fair*; this classic image of reversed order ('Let's have the giddy world turn'd the heeles upward') is allowed to infiltrate with a delicate appropriateness. The criticism which Jonson levelled at Shakespeare may now be levelled at him, for each playwright is complying with the tyranny of popular dramatic taste; as so often in the play, the judge turns out to be an offender himself. The wry, somewhat angry paradox is delineated with some sophistication. Such sophistication is of quite a different order from the 'noise' and 'sport' which the Scrivener promises to the groundlings, and helps to encourage at this early stage an awareness that the comedy is appealing simultaneously at two different levels. This awareness persists throughout the play itself; and we cannot help but remember Jonson's implications about the literary taste of his age as we hear Littlewit, Overdo, Leatherhead, and Busy discourse in their different ways about the vanity of learning, of poetry, and of the stage itself.

— Ian Donaldson, The World Upside-Down (Oxford: Clarendon Press, 1970): pp. 46–48.

RICHARD ALLEN CAVE ON THE INDUCTION SCENE AND THE PUPPET SHOW

[Richard Allen Cave is Professor of Drama and Theatre Arts in the University of London at Royal Holloway and Bedford New College. He is the author of *Ben Jonson* (English Dramatists), *The White Devil and the Duchess of Malfi, Ben Jonson and the Theatre: A Critical and Practical Introduction, A Study of the Novels of George Moore, The Romantic Theatre* and *New British Drama in Performance on the London Stage, 1970–1985* as well as being a co-author or editor for numerous other works. In this excerpt, Cave analyzes the Induction scene and the puppet show, arguing that through each Jonson challenges audience members to consider their role as active moral judges of the action.]

In the play scene from *Bartholomew Fair* there are at least fourteen characters on-stage as spectators in the booth or as manipulators. ⟨. . .⟩ The small stature of the puppet-performers (compensated for by their extravagantly vigorous activity) allows us to watch both the play-within-the-play and the groups of on-stage spectators with ease and with rapt attention. Once again we have been placed by Jonson in a position where we can watch and judge the effect of performance: as an audience we are required to study an audience. ⟨...⟩

⟨...⟩ Repeatedly throughout *Bartholomew Fair* Jonson devises tactics, alienation effects, to make his audience conscious of their complex and creative relation to the play in performance. The puppet play is in fact the best and most intricate of a carefully graduated sequence of strategies, which simultaneously entertain while inviting us to explore our laughter and so probe deeply into the psychology of performance and audience-response. ⟨...⟩

The play begins with one of Jonson's funniest and most inventive Inductions that wittily intimates all the themes that are to be explored later in depth. ⟨...⟩ The prompter ⟨...⟩ officiously instructs the scrivener to read an indenture that sets out certain 'articles of agreement' between Jonson and the audience in which the dramatist guarantees us our money's worth of enjoyment providing we fulfil certain conditions in our turn: that throughout we will be completely at ease with ourselves; that we will be quite open to the experience offered us and not churlishly hope for a play written either to worn-out or to currently modish conventions; that we should accept that any play will establish its own particular decorum and related criteria defining verisimilitude, so we should not be disappointed if we fail to get romantic transformations after the fashion recently set by Shakespeare; and, if we should sense a satirical impulse at work in the comedy, we should not suppose it directed at specific individuals. With remarkable economy of stage-time Jonson has set our minds thinking about questions of dramatic realism and decorum of style and their relation to modes of perception and judgement. He warns us that we are not going to be allowed to rest apathetically content with a play written to popular formulae: we have our contribution to bring to the performance, which he trusts will be a generous engagement, not a critical superiority. He presents this material through three contrasting voices: one earthy, one primly condescending and one flatly impersonal and legal. This perfectly demonstrates Jonson's theme—that judgement is subjective, impressionistic, and immediately reflects on the character of the speaker.

Hanging uneasily over the Induction, giving an edge to the laughter, is the awareness that judgement can lead to censure or correction. What if the articles of agreement are broken? ⟨...⟩ It is noticeable that though the threat of correction is always present in the play (Justice Overdo vows to castigate richly all enormities he detects at the fair), it never actually materialises. ⟨. . .⟩ Noticeably the recent productions which reviewers have found confusing tend to be ones where the director has omitted the Induction. Given a play of the length of *Bartholomew Fair* that is an understandable but fatal decision, since as a prologue it subtly establishes the linguistic and thematic parameters within which the ensuing comedy will work. Most importantly the Induction alerts an audience's wits to their relation to the play being performed: the articles of agreement define our role as seriously active not passive. *Bartholomew Fair* is to be an exercising of our moral imaginations.

—Richard Allen Cave, *Ben Jonson* (Houndmills, England: Macmillan Education, Ltd., 1991): pp. 95, 97–100.

Works by Ben Jonson

The Case Is Altered	pr.	1597
The Isle of Dogs (with Thomas Nashe)	pr.	1597
Every Man in His Humour	pr.	1598
Hot Anger Soon Cold (with Henry Chettle & Henry Porter)	pr.	1598
Every Man Out of His Humour	pr.	1599
Robert the Second, King of Scots (with Chettle & Decker)	pr.	1599
The Page of Plymouth (with Thomas Decker)	pr.	1599
Cynthia's Revels: Or, The Fountain of Self-Love	pr.	c. 1600–1601
Poems		1601
Poetaster: Or, His Arraignment	pr.	1601
Sejanus His Fall	pr.	1603
Eastward Ho! (with George Chapman & John Marston)	pr.	1605 pb. 1605
Volpone: Or, The Fox	pr.	1605
Epicoene: Or, The Silent Woman	pr.	1609
The Alchemist	pr.	1610
Catiline His Conspiracy	pr.	1611 pb. 1611
Bartholomew Fair	pr.	1614
Epigrams		1616
The Devil Is an Ass	pr.	1616
The Forest		1616
The Workes of Benjamin Jonson		1616

The Staple of News	pr.	1626
The New Inn: Or, *The Light Heart*	pr.	1629
The Magnetic Lady: Or, *Humours Reconciled*	pr.	1632
A Tale of a Tub	pr.	1633
Horace His Art of Poetry		1640
The English Grammer		1640
The Sad Shepherd: Or, *A Tale of Robin Hood*	pb.	1640
Underwoods		1640
The Works of Benjamin Jonson		1640–1641
Timber: Or, Discoveries Made *upon Men and Matter*		1641

Works About
Ben Jonson

Adams, Robert M., ed. Ben Jonson's *Plays and Masques*. New York: W. W. Norton, 1979.

Barish, Jonas A. "The Double Plot in *Volpone*" in *Ben Jonson*. Ed. Harold Bloom. New York: Chelsea House Publishers, 1987.

————. *Ben Jonson and the Language of Prose Comedy*. Cambridge: Harvard University Press, 1960.

————, ed. *Ben Jonson: A Collection of Critical Essays*. Englewood Cliffs: Prentice Hall, 1963

Barton, Anne. *Ben Jonson, Dramatist*. Cambridge: Cambridge University Press, 1984.

Bryant, J. A. " Jonson's Revision of *Every Man in His Humour*," *Studies in Philology* 59, 1962.

Cave, Richard Allen. *Ben Jonson*. Houndmills, England: Macmillan Education, Ltd., 1991.

Coleridge, Samuel. *Coleridge's Literary Criticism*. London: Henry Frowde, 1908.

————. *Lectures and Notes on Shakespeare and Other English Poets*. London: George Bell & Sons, 1893.

Craig, D. H., ed. *Ben Jonson: The Critical Heritage, 1599–1798*. London: Routledge, 1990.

Donaldson, Ian. *Jonson's Magic Houses: Essays in Interpretation*. Oxford: Clarendon Press, 1997.

————. *The World Upside Down*. Oxford: Oxford University Press, 1970.

Dryden, John. *Of Dramatic Poesy and Other Critical Essays*. London: Dent, 1962.

Ellis-Fermor, Una. *The Jacobean Drama: An Interpretation*. New York: Vintage Books, 1964.

Empson, William. "Volpone" in *Ben Jonson's* Volpone, or the Fox. Ed. Harold Bloom. New York: Chelsea House Publishers, 1988.

Harp, Richard, ed. *Ben Jonson's Plays and Masques,* 2nd ed. New York: W. W. Norton, 2001.

Hazlitt, William. *Lectures on the English Comic Writers.* New York: Russell & Russell, 1969.

Herford, C. H. and Simpson, Percy. *Ben Jonson: Volumes I & II, The Man and His Work, The Second Volume.* London: Oxford University Press, 1925.

Kernan, Alvin B. *The Cankered Muse.* New Haven: Yale University Press, 1959.

———. Introduction to *Ben Jonson:* The Alchemist. New Haven: Yale University Press, 1974.

———. *Two Renaissance Mythmakers: Christopher Marlowe and Ben Jonson.* Baltimore: Johns Hopkins University Press, 1977

Knights, L. C. *Drama and Society in the Age of Jonson.* London: Chatto & Windus, 1937

Leggatt, A. *Ben Jonson: His Vision and His Art.* New York: Methuen, 1981

Levin, Harry. Introduction to *Ben Jonson: Selected Works.* New York: Random House, 1938.

———. "Jonson's Metempsychosis." *Philological Quarterly* 22 (1943): 231–39.

Orgel, Stephen. *The Illusion of Power: Political Theatre in the English Renaissance.* Berkeley and Los Angeles: University of California Press, 1975.

Ornstein, Robert. *The Moral Vision of Jacobean Tragedy.* Madison: University of Wisconsin Press, 1965.

Partridge, Edward B., ed. Introduction to *Bartholomew Fair,* by Ben Jonson. Lincoln, Nebraska: University of Nebraska Press, 1964.

———. *The Broken Compass: A Study of the Major Comedies of Ben Jonson.* New York: Columbia University Press, 1958.

Riggs, David. *Ben Jonson: A Life.* Cambridge, Massachusetts: Harvard University Press, 1989.

Salingar, Leo. *Dramatic Form in Shakespeare and the Jacobeans.* Cambridge: Cambridge University Press, 1986.

Swinburne, Algernon Charles. *A Study of Ben Jonson.* London: Chatto & Windus, 1889.

Trussler, Simon. Commentary in *Every Man in His Humour,* by Ben Jonson. London: Methuen, 1986.

Watson, Robert N. Introduction to *Every Man in His Humour,* by Ben Jonson. London: A & C Black, 1998.

Index of
Themes and Ideas

20, 32–34, 35; Thomas Kitely in, 21–23, 25, 28, 36; Kno'well in, 20, 21, 22, 23, 24, 30, 35; Edward Kno'well in, 20, 21, 22, 24; Master Matthew in, 20, 21, 22, 23, 25, 29, 30, 35, 36; plot summary of, 20–23; and pretense and realism, 34–36; revisions of, 20, 29–30; Master Stephen in, 21, 24, 29, 34, 35–36; strengths and weaknesses in, 28–29; Wellbred in, 20, 21, 22, 24

EVERY MAN OUT OF HIS HUMOR, 10, 17, 30

ISLE OF DOGS, 17

JONSON, BEN: and art as hard work for, 26–28; biography of, 16–19; on low humor and didactic functions of comedy, 84–85; and Shakespeare, 9–11, 26–28, 31–32, 68, 74–76, 87–89, 94; and Virgil, 75

MAGNETIC LADY, THE, 19

NEW INN, THE, 19

POETASTER, 10, 17

SEJANUS, 9, 17, 18

TALE OF A TUB, A, 19

VOLPONE, 18, 37–58; *The Alchemist versus,* 66–67, 69–72; Androgino in, 44; Avvocati in, 39–40, 43, 46; Bonario in, 38–39, 40, 43–44, 46, 66; Castrone in, 40, 43; Celia in, 12, 38–39, 40, 44, 46, 48, 52, 53, 54, 66; characters in, 42–44; as comedy approaching tragedy, 45–46; Corbaccio in, 37, 38, 39, 40, 41, 42, 46, 53, 56; Corvino in, 37, 38, 39, 40, 41, 43, 46, 56; critical views on, 9, 11–15, 45–58, 66–67, 69–72, 75, 86, 93; and Jonson's affection for Volpone, 50–52; as Jonson's triumph, 11–15; moral aspects of, 47–48; Mosca in, 11, 12, 37, 38, 39, 40, 42, 51, 54, 56, 57, 58, 71–72; Nano in, 40, 43; Peregrine in, 38, 39, 40, 43, 55; plot summary of, 37–41; and subplot, 54–56; Volpone in, 11–15, 37, 38, 39, 40–41, 42, 46, 48–54, 55, 56–58, 66, 69–71, 90; and Volpone's antics as quest for elixir of life, 52–54; and Volpone's speeches as Scoto of Mantua, 38, 48–50; and Volpone's vitalism, 56–58; Voltore in, 37, 39, 40, 42, 46, 56; Fine Lady Would-Be in, 38, 39, 40, 44, 54–56; Sir Politic Would-Be in, 38, 39, 40, 43, 54–56